ISLAMIC HISTORY

THE ISLAMIC WORLD

ISLAMIC HISTORY

EDITED BY LAURA ETHEREDGE, ASSISTANT EDITOR,
MIDDLE EAST GEOGRAPHY

Britannica®
Educational Publishing

IN ASSOCIATION WITH

ROSEN
EDUCATIONAL SERVICES

Published in 2010 by Britannica Educational Publishing
(a trademark of Encyclopædia Britannica, Inc.)
in association with Rosen Educational Services, LLC
29 East 21st Street, New York, NY 10010.

First Edition

Britannica Educational Publishing
Michael I. Levy: Executive Editor
Marilyn L. Barton: Senior Coordinator, Production Control
Steven Bosco: Director, Editorial Technologies
Lisa S. Braucher: Senior Producer and Data Editor
Yvette Charboneau: Senior Copy Editor
Kathy Nakamura: Manager, Media Acquisition
Laura Etheredge: Assistant Editor, Middle East Geography

Rosen Educational Services
Hope Lourie Killcoyne: Senior Editor and Project Manager
Joanne Randolph: Editor
Nelson Sá: Art Director
Nicole Russo: Designer
Introduction by Alexandra Hanson-Harding

Library of Congress Cataloging-in-Publication Data

Islamic history / edited by Laura S. Etheredge.—1st ed.
    p. cm.—(The Islamic world)
"In association with Rosen Educational Services."
Includes index.
ISBN 978-1-61530-021-1 (library binding)
1. Islamic countries—History. 2. Civilization, Islamic. 3. Islam—History. I. Etheredge, Laura S.
DS35.63.I84 2010
909'.09767—dc22

                                                    2009037874

Manufactured in the United States of America

On the cover: The Ka'bah is a small shrine near the centre of the Great Mosque in Mecca.
Considered by Muslims worldwide to be the most sacred spot on Earth, it is the place to
which Muslims orient themselves during daily prayers. *Shutterstock.com*

CONTENTS

Introduction   10

Chapter One:
The Precursors of Islam
(c. 3000 BCE–500 CE)   19
The Rise of Agrarian-Based
    Citied Societies   21
Cultural Core Areas of the
    Settled World   23
    The Nile-to-Oxus Region   23
    The Arabian Peninsula   25

Chapter Two:
Formation and Orientation
(c. 500–634)   29
The City of Mecca: Centre of
    Trade and Religion   29
    Mecca Under the
    Quraysh Clans   30
    New Social Patterns Among the
    Meccans and Their Neighbours 33
The Prophet Muhammad   35
    Muhammad's Years in Mecca   35
    Muhammad's Emigration
    to Yathrib (Medina)   39
    Battle of Badr   43
    Battle of the Ditch   45
Islam at Muhammad's Death   46
Abu Bakr's Succession   48
    Riddah   49

Chapter Three:
Conversion and
Crystallization (634–870)   52

Social and Cultural
    Transformations   52
'Umar I's Succession   55
    The Spirit of Conquest Under
    'Umar I   55
    Forging the Link of Activism
    with Faithfulness   56
'Uthman's Succession and Policies   58
    Discontent in 'Uthman's Reign   58
    Intra-Muslim Conflicts   60
The Four *Fitnah*s   61
    The First *Fitnah*   61
    The Second *Fitnah*   63
    Battle of Siffin   64
    The Emergent Islamic
    Civilization   67
    Dome of the Rock   68
    The Third *Fitnah*   73
    Sunnis and Shi'ites   77
    The 'Abbasids   80
    Harun al-Rashid   82
    Shari'ah   85
    The Fourth *Fitnah*   87
    Al-Bukhari   91

Chapter Four:
Fragmentation and
Florescence (870–1041)   93
The Rise of Competitive Regions   93
Andalusia, the Maghrib, and
    Sub-Saharan Africa   95
    'Abd al-Rahman I   96
Egypt, Syria, and the Holy Cities   100
    The Fatimid Dynasty   100
    Al-Azhar University   101
    The Hamdanid Dynasty   103

Iraq   104
    Cultural Flowering in Iraq   104
    Al-Tabari   105
    The Buyid Dynasty   108
Iran, Afghanistan, and India   113
    The Samanids   113
    The Ghaznavids   114
The Decline of the Caliphate and
    Rise of Emirates   117

Chapter Five:
Migration and
Renewal (1041–1405)   119
Turks   120
    Seljuq Turks   120
    Policies of Nizam al-Mulk   122
    Nizam al-Mulk   124
    Tariqah Fellowships   126
Franks   127
    The Call for the Crusades   127
    Effects of the Crusades
    in Syria   128
    Saladin   131
Mongols   133
    Genghis Khan   134
    First Mongol Incursions   135
    Conversion of Mongols
    to Islam   137
    Ascent of the Ottoman Turks 142
    Timur's Efforts to Restore
    Mongol Power   143
    Timur   144
Arabs   146
Imazighen   146
    The Sanhajah Confederation 147
    The Almoravid Dynasty   148

The Almohad Dynasty   151
Continued Spread of Islamic
Influence   152

Chapter Six:
Consolidation and
Expansion (1405–1683)   156
Ottomans   159
    Continuation of Ottoman Rule 159
    Reign of Süleyman I   160
    Süleyman I   161
    The Extent of Ottoman
    Administration   163
Safavids   165
    Expansion in Iran and Beyond 166
    Shah 'Abbas I   168
    Decline of Central Authority 170
Indo-Timurids (Mughals)   170
    Foundation by Babur   170
    Reign of Akbar   172
    Continuation of the Empire 174
    Shah Jahan   176
Trans-Saharan Islam   178
Indian Ocean Islam   181

Chapter Seven:
Islamic History from 1683 to the
Present: Reform, Dependency,
and Recovery   184
Pre-colonial Reform and
    Experimentation (1683 to 1818) 186
The Rise of British Colonialism
    to the End of the Ottoman
    Empire   190
Islam and Nationalism in the Age of
    Globalization (The Early 20th
    Century to the Present)   193

Reform and Revival in the
Colonial Period   193
Rashid Rida   195
Nationalism: Postcolonial
States and Islam   197
Muslim Brotherhood   198
Islamist Movements from
the 1960s   200
Ruhollah Khomeini   202
The Mainstreaming of Islamist
Movements   205
Dimensions of the Islamic
Revival   207
Islam and Globalization: The
Age of Mobility   209

Glossary   214
For Further Reading   216
Index   218

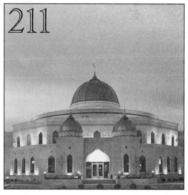

INTRODUCTION

A round 610 CE, a merchant meditating in a cave outside Mecca began to receive a series of revelations. From that vision grew Islam, one of the world's great religions. What Islam's prophet, Muhammad, began gave rise to a number of mighty empires. Islam proved to be such a powerful force that today, 1,400 years after a vision appeared to the Prophet, it is the world's second largest religion. With more than one billion adherents, Islam has deep roots in the Asia, Africa, and Europe. More than half of today's Muslims live in Asia alone, from Turkey to Indonesia. Worldwide, a tremendous variety of people follow Islam—from blue-eyed Bosnians to African Americans to the Uighurs of western China. After fourteen centuries, Islam remains one of the world's fastest-growing faiths.

But Islam, by virtue of extremist acts that pressed its name into the consciousness of many as the 21st century was just beginning, faces a new hurdle. With the terrorist attacks of September 11, 2001 in the United States—and subsequent attacks in Bali, London, Madrid, and elsewhere—radical Islam seized global attention. The images, headlines, and aftermath of each attack indelibly linked those events with the name of Islam. In spite of the attention seized by Muslim extremists in recent history, however, the broader history of Islam is one of astonishing growth and great achievement. Islam itself is complex and multifaceted, and its faithful have, over centuries, been massively prolific in works of science, philosophy, theology, and the arts. From the luminous symmetry of the Taj Mahal to algebraic equations, from the tales of *The Thousand and One Nights* to the collected works of poets such as Rumi or Hafiz, Islam has provided a rich tapestry of contributions to world culture.

What binds Muslims? Muslims believe in one God and affirm Muhammad as His prophet. They hold Islam to be the third revelation of monotheism—after Judaism and Christianity—and as such revere many of the prophets honoured in Jewish and Christian tradition, including Abraham, Noah, Moses, and Jesus. Muslims also share several spiritual guides. One is the Qur'an, the sacred scripture of Islam revealed by God to Muhammad and, for all Muslims, the very word of God. Another is the Hadith, the record of the traditions or sayings of the Prophet, revered by Muslims as a major source of religious law and moral guidance and second only to the authority of the Qur'an.

Incumbent upon every Muslim are five duties known collectively as the Five Pillars of Islam. First among these is the recitation of a profession of faith called the *shahadah* ("There is no god but God and Muhammad is His prophet"), which must be recited by a Muslim at least once in his or her lifetime. In addition, observant Muslims say prayers five times a day, give to charity, fast during the holy month of Ramadan, and, if they are able, make a pilgrimage to Mecca, Muhammad's birthplace. In addition to the Five Pillars, many Muslims around the world also study the Qur'an.

In this book, you will learn why Arabia was such fertile ground for the emergence of a new faith. In its prehistorical period (3000 BCE–500 CE), the dry Arabian Peninsula, most of which was unfavourable for settled agriculture, derived great wealth from its prime location at an important trade crossroads: caravans crisscrossed the desert bringing goods from China, India, and Africa in the East to trade as far as Spain in the West. For hundreds of years, Arabia's residents served as middlemen in this trade; thus, although agricultural opportunity may have been limited, commercial opportunity was almost limitless.

In 570, Muhammad was born in Mecca, already an important Arabian trading and religious centre, in what is known as Islam's formation and orientation period (500-634 CE). Muhammad was a serious young man whose parents had died when he was young; he was raised for a short time by his grandfather, and then by his uncle, Abu Talib. He later worked for a wealthy businesswoman named Khadijah, whom he married at age 25. Full of spiritual questions, Muhammad often sought the solitude of the desert to think and pray. It was on one such trip that the 40-year-old Muhammad had a revelation. The angel Gabriel came to him, saying three times "Recite!" and told Muhammad that he was the messenger of God. Muhammad went home, relating to Khadijah what had happened. Soon she became Islam's first convert.

The revelations persisted, and after several years of preaching to his family and friends, Muhammad started delivering his revelations to others in the form of public recitations. Although a number of prominent Meccans became believers, many others harassed his supporters, forcing some of them into a period of exile. During this difficult time, Muhammad faced the deaths of two of his dearest companions: Khadijah, his wife and confidant, as well as his beloved uncle and protector, Abu Talib. And yet, in spite of the challenges, Muhammad's flock continued to grow. In 622 he moved his followers in small, inconspicuous groups to the city of Yathrib (Medina) in an emigration known as the Hijrah. In Medina Muhammad established Islam as a religious and social order. From there, Muhammad later led campaigns against his opponents, including Mecca; by 629 he was able to lead his followers on the first peaceful pilgrimage to that city. He continued to receive revelations until his death in 632.

After the Prophet Muhammad's passing, the Muslim faithful learned to survive as a community in the period of conversion and crystallization (634–870 CE). First, four "rightly guided" caliphs, all friends or relatives of Muhammad, ruled from 632 to 661. These leaders stretched Islam's borders by taking over Palestine, Egypt, Syria, and parts of Iraq. They also organized the government.

One important event was a controversy over 'Ali, the pious cousin and son-in-law of Muhammad, who was the last of these caliphs. 'Ali faced many difficulties, including the opposition of Mu'awiyah, the governor of Syria. But 'Ali had supporters, too, called the Shi'at 'Ali, or Partisans of 'Ali. In 661, 'Ali was murdered. After 'Ali's assassination, Mu'awiyah assumed the caliphate, founding the Umayyad dynasty. That injustice—and later the murder of 'Ali's son al-Husayn by Umayyad troops—angered the Shi'ites. They opposed the Umayyads' more secular rule and decided to follow spiritual leaders called imams. Thus began a separation between two branches of Islam: the Sunni, who make up 85 percent of Muslims today, and the Shi'ah, who constitute the remainder.

Meanwhile, the Umayyad empire flourished. The Umayyads, who ruled from Damascus, Syria, expanded their empire all the way from the western Mediterranean into Central Asia. They also made use of the *dhimmi* system in managing their heterogenous empire. Under this arrangement, Jews and Christians were not forced to convert to Islam, but they did have to pay a special tax for living in the empire. This way, the empire encouraged but did not force religious conversion. In fact, most of the future Islamic empires had systems in place that made room for religious minorities in their midst. In many of these empires, Christians and Jews would even have privileged places in the government and the military. In

750 a new dynasty, the 'Abbasids, overthrew the Umayyads and began to rule from a new capital city, Baghdad.

During the period of fragmentation and florescence (flowering) that took place between 870 and 1041, the 'Abbasid empire became a centre for art and science. After Chinese papermakers were captured in battle in 751, Muslim artisans learned how to make paper for books. Literature spread quickly. Great works were translated from ancient Greek, Sanskrit, Syriac, and other languages into Arabic. These new ideas encouraged the development of schools of philosophy (*falsafah*, adapting the word from Greek). Muslim scholars made contributions to the sciences in fields such as algebra, astronomy, botany, chemistry, and medicine. They became experts at mapmaking and navigation. Over time, regional dynasties began to develop, too, such as the Fatimids, who captured Egypt and created a new capital, Cairo.

Although Islam was blooming, it faced obstacles and hostilities that ultimately caused it to redirect and thrive in new ways. During the period of migration and renewal, from 1041 to 1405, broad in-migration and assimilation played an especially crucial role. As part of this trend, a number of Muslim cities were attacked by outsiders. Christian Crusaders captured Jerusalem, a city holy to Christians, Muslims, and Jews, in 1099. The Crusaders were finally forced from Jerusalem by Saladin, a powerful Muslim leader, in 1187. In 1258, the Mongols—pagan, horse-riding tribes of the Central Asian steppe—invaded Baghdad, where they slaughtered hundreds of thousands of residents and terminated the caliphate. Ironically, after several generations, the Mongols themselves converted to Islam, spreading the faith across their vast empire.

Three powerful empires rose during the period of consolidation and expansion (1405–1683). Babur, a descendent of Mongol leader Genghis Khan, started taking over India in 1519, founding the Mughal dynasty. At its greatest extent, the Mughal empire covered most of the Indian subcontinent. Mughal ruler Shah Jahan had the Taj Mahal, one of the architectural wonders of the world, built in memory of the favourite of his three wives.

By contrast, the Shi'ite Safavid dynasty had its origins in a Sufi brotherhood in northwestern Iran. After winning the support of local Turkish tribesmen and other disaffected groups, the Safavids were able to expand throughout Iran and into parts of Iraq.

Meanwhile, in what is now Turkey, the Ottoman Empire was on the march. The Ottoman dynasty, which had started at the turn of the 14th century, conquered lands in the Middle East and in Europe, including Hungary, Serbia, Romania, and Bosnia. In 1453 the Ottomans captured Constantinople from the Byzantine Empire and turned it into the new capital, Istanbul. The Ottoman Empire's trade ships controlled much of the Mediterranean Sea. The Ottomans had a sophisticated culture and made alliances with European powers such as France and Great Britain. Then, in 1683, the Ottomans reached a limit. In that year, they invaded Austria, penetrating all the way to Vienna, where their ambitious campaign failed. It was a turning point, and a telling marker for the future.

As the Islamic world entered its next phase, reform, dependency, and recovery (1683 to the present), it faced a new challenge—the rising power of Europe.

In the 1800s the British took over India as a colony, finally snuffing out the crumbling Mughal empire. The Ottoman Empire survived longer, but over time it weakened as well. As it did, colonial powers such as France and Britain took control, both directly and indirectly, of more and more territory in Africa, Asia, and the Middle East.

Western powers grew increasingly interested in influencing the Middle East when they learned of the vast stores of oil that lay underneath such countries as Iran, Iraq, and Saudi Arabia. Eventually, colonized lands became new countries, in some cases more constructs than organic nations, with arbitrary boundaries and markedly different groups of people suddenly designated as countrymen. Such acts led to many questions about what kind of identity should matter most—national or religious.

As you read this book you will learn much more about the Islamic world. You will have the opportunity to explore the perils and promise of great empires, to discover a profound and diverse cultural heritage, and to learn what unites and separates different branches of the Islamic faith. And you will gain a new perspective on one of the world's greatest and most enduring religions.

CHAPTER 1

THE PRECURSORS OF ISLAM (c. 3000 BCE–500 CE)

Adherence to Islam is a global phenomenon: Muslims predominate in some 30 to 40 countries, from the Atlantic eastward to the Pacific and along a belt that stretches across northern Africa into Central Asia and south to the northern regions of the Indian subcontinent. Although many in the West consider Arabs and Muslims synonymous, Arabs account for fewer than one-fifth of all Muslims, more than half of whom live east of Karachi, Pakistan. Despite the absence of large-scale Islamic political entities, the Islamic faith continues to expand, by some estimates faster than any other major religion.

A very broad perspective is required to explain the history of today's Islamic world. This approach must enlarge upon conventional political or dynastic divisions to draw a comprehensive picture of the stages by which successive Muslim communities, throughout Islam's 14 centuries, encountered and incorporated new peoples so as to produce an international religion and civilization.

In general, events referred to here are dated according to the Gregorian calendar, and eras are designated BCE (before the Common Era or Christian Era) and CE (Common Era or Christian Era), terms which are equivalent to BC (before Christ) and AD (Latin: *anno Domini*). In some cases the Muslim reckoning of the Islamic era is used, indicated by AH (Latin: *anno Hegirae*). The Islamic era begins with the date of Muhammad's emigration (Hijrah) to Medina, which corresponds to July 16, 622 CE, in the Gregorian calendar.

The term *Islamic* refers to Islam as a religion. The term *Islamicate* refers to the social and cultural complex that is historically associated with Islam and the Muslims, even when found among non-Muslims. *Islamdom* refers to that complex of societies in which the Muslims and their faith have been prevalent and socially dominant.

The prehistory of Islamdom is the history of central Afro-Eurasia from Hammurabi of Babylon to the Achaemenid Cyrus II in Persia to Alexander the Great to the Sasanian emperor Nushirvan to Muhammad in Arabia; or, in a Muslim view, from Adam to Noah to Abraham to Moses to Jesus to Muhammad. The potential for Muslim empire building was established with the rise of the earliest civilizations in western Asia. It was refined with the emergence and spread of what have been called the region's Axial Age religions—Abrahamic, centred on the Hebrew patriarch Abraham, and Mazdean, focused on the Iranian deity Ahura Mazda—and their later relative, Christianity. It was facilitated by the expansion of trade from eastern Asia to the Mediterranean and by the political changes thus effected. The Muslims were heirs to the ancient Egyptians, Babylonians, Persians, Hebrews, even the Greeks and Indians; the societies they created bridged time and space, from ancient to modern and from east to west.

THE RISE OF AGRARIAN-BASED CITIED SOCIETIES

In the 7th century CE a coalition of Arab groups, some sedentary and some migratory, inside and outside the Arabian Peninsula, seized political and fiscal control in western Asia, specifically of the lands between the Nile and Oxus (Amu Darya) rivers—territory formerly controlled by the Byzantines in the west and the Sasanians in the east. The factors that surrounded and directed their accomplishment had begun to coalesce long before, with the emergence of agrarian-based cited societies in western Asia in the 4th millennium BCE. The rise of complex agrarian-based societies, such as Sumer, out of a subsistence agricultural and pastoralist environment, involved

This ziggurat, a pyramidal temple, dates back to 2113 BCE. Standing more than 50 feet (17 metres) high, the temple is in the ancient city of Ur, located in modern-day Iraq. Karim Sahib/AFP/Getty Images

the founding of cities, the extension of citied power over surrounding villages, and the interaction of both with pastoralists.

This type of social organization offered new possibilities. Agricultural production and intercity trading, particularly in luxury goods, increased. Some individuals were able to take advantage of the manual labour of others to amass enough wealth to patronize a wide range of arts and crafts. Of these, a few were able to establish territorial monarchies and foster religious institutions with wider appeal. Gradually the familiar troika of court, temple, and market emerged. The new ruling groups cultivated skills for administering and integrating non-kin-related groups. They benefited from the increased use of writing and, in many cases, from the adoption of a single writing system, such as the cuneiform, for administrative use. New institutions, such as coinage, territorial deities, royal priesthoods, and standing armies, further enhanced their power.

In such town-and-country complexes the pace of change quickened enough so that a well-placed individual might see the effects of his actions in his own lifetime and be stimulated to self-criticism and moral reflection of an unprecedented sort. The religion of these new social entities reflected and supported the new social environments. Unlike the religions of small groups, the religions of complex societies focused on deities, such as Marduk, Isis, or Mithra, whose appeal was not limited to one small area or group and whose powers were much less fragmented. The relationship of earthly existence to the afterlife became more problematic, as evidenced by the elaborate death rites of pharaonic Egypt. Individual religious action began to compete with communal worship and ritual; sometimes it promised spiritual transformation and transcendence of a new sort, as illustrated in the pan-Mediterranean mystery religions. Yet large-scale organization had introduced social and economic injustices that rulers and religions could address but not resolve. To many, an absolute ruler uniting a plurality of ethnic, religious, and interest groups offered the best hope of justice.

CULTURAL CORE AREAS OF THE SETTLED WORLD

By the middle of the 1st millennium BCE the settled world had crystallized into four cultural core areas: Mediterranean, Nile-to-Oxus, Indic, and East Asian. The Nile-to-Oxus, the future core of Islamdom, was the least cohesive and the most complicated. Whereas each of the other regions developed a single language of high culture—Greek, Sanskrit, and Chinese, respectively—the Nile-to-Oxus region was a linguistic palimpsest of Irano-Semitic languages of several sorts: Aramaic, Syriac (eastern or Iranian Aramaic), and Middle Persian (the language of eastern Iran).

THE NILE-TO-OXUS REGION

In addition to its various linguistic groups, the Nile-to-Oxus region also differed in climate and ecology. It lay at the centre of a vast arid zone stretching across Afro-Eurasia from the Sahara to the Gobi. It favoured those who could deal with aridity—not only states that could control flooding (as in Egypt) or maintain irrigation (as in Mesopotamia) but also pastoralists and oasis dwellers. Although its agricultural potential was severely limited, its commercial possibilities were virtually unlimited. Located at the crossroads of the trans-Asian trade and blessed with numerous natural transit points, the region offered special social and economic prominence to its merchants.

The period from 800 to 200 BCE has been called the Axial Age because of its pivotal importance for the history of religion and culture. The world's first religions of salvation developed in the four core areas. From these traditions—for example, Judaism, Mazdeism, Buddhism, and Confucianism—derived all later forms of high religion, including Christianity and Islam. Unlike the religions that surrounded their formation, the Axial Age religions concentrated transcendent power into one locus, be it symbolized theistically or nontheistically. Their radically dualistic cosmology posited another realm, totally unlike the earthly realm and capable of challenging and replacing ordinary earthly values. The individual was challenged to adopt the right relationship with that "other" realm, so as to transcend mortality by earning a final resting place, or to escape the immortality guaranteed by rebirth by achieving annihilation of earthly attachment.

In the Nile-to-Oxus region two major traditions arose during the Axial Age: the Abrahamic in the west and the Mazdean in the east. Because they required exclusive allegiance through an individual confession of faith in a just and judging deity, they are called confessional religions. This deity was a unique all-powerful creator who remained active in history, and each event in the life of every individual was meaningful in terms of the judgment of God at the end of time. The universally applicable truth of these new religions was expressed in sacred writings. The traditions reflected the mercantile environment in which they were formed in their special concern for fairness, honesty, covenant keeping, moderation, law and order, accountability, and the rights of ordinary human beings. These values were always potentially incompatible with the elitism and absolutism of courtly circles. Most often, as in the example of the Achaemenian Empire, the conflict was expressed in rebellion against the crown or was adjudicated by viewing kingship as the guarantor of divine justice.

Although modern Western historiography has projected an East-West dichotomy onto ancient times, Afro-Eurasian continuities and interactions were well established by the Axial Age and persisted throughout premodern times. The history of Islamdom cannot be understood without reference to them. Through Alexander's conquests in the 4th century BCE in three of the four core areas, the Irano-Semitic cultures of the Nile-to-Oxus region were permanently overlaid with Hellenistic elements, and a link was forged between the Indian subcontinent and Iran. By the 3rd century CE, crosscutting movements like Gnosticism and Manichaeism integrated individuals from disparate cultures. Similarly organized large, land-based empires with official religions existed in all parts of the settled world. The Christian Roman Empire was locked in conflict with its counterpart to the east, the Zoroastrian-Mazdean Sasanian empire. Another Christian empire in East Africa, the Abyssinian, was involved alternately with each of the others. In the context of these regional interrelationships, inhabitants of Arabia made their fateful entrance into international political, religious, and economic life.

THE ARABIAN PENINSULA

The Arabian Peninsula consists of a large central arid zone punctuated by oases, wells, and small seasonal streams and bounded in the south by well-watered lands that are generally thin, sometimes mountainous coastal strips. To the north of the peninsula are the irrigated agricultural areas of Syria and Iraq, the site of large-scale states from the 4th millennium BCE. As early as the beginning of the 1st millennium BCE the southwest corner of Arabia, the Yemen, was also divided into settled kingdoms. Their language was a South Arabian Semitic dialect, and their culture bore some affinity to Semitic societies in the Fertile Crescent. By the beginning of the Common Era (the 1st century AD in the Christian calendar), the major occupants of the habitable parts of the arid centre were known as Arabs. They were Semitic-speaking tribes of settled, semi-settled, and fully migratory peoples who drew their name and apparently their identity from what the camel-herding Bedouin pastoralists among them called themselves: *'arab*.

Until the beginning of the 3rd century CE the greatest economic and political power in the peninsula rested in the relatively independent kingdoms of the Yemen. The Yemenis, with a knowledge of the monsoon winds, had evolved an exceptionally long and profitable trade route from East Africa across the Red Sea and from India across the Indian Ocean up through the peninsula into Iraq and Syria, where it joined older Phoenician routes across the Mediterranean and into the Iberian Peninsula. Their power depended on their ability to protect islands discovered in the Indian Ocean and to control the straits of Hormuz and Aden. It also depended on the Bedouin caravanners who guided and protected the caravans that carried the trade northward to Arab entrepôts like Petra and Palmyra. Participation in this trade was in turn an important source of power for tribal Arabs, whose livelihood otherwise depended on a combination of intergroup raiding, agriculture, and animal husbandry.

By the 3rd century, however, external developments began to impinge. In the early 3rd century, Ardashir I founded the Sasanian empire in Fars. Within 70 years the Sasanian state was at war with Rome, a conflict that was to last up to Islamic times. The Roman Empire was reorganized under Constantine the Great, with the adoption of a new faith, Christianity, and a new capital, Constantinople. These changes exacerbated the competition with the Sasanian empire and resulted in the spreading of Christianity into Egypt and Abyssinia and the encouraging of missionizing in Arabia itself. In Arabia Christians encountered Jews who had been settling there since the 1st century, as well as Arabs who had converted to Judaism. By the beginning of the 4th century the rulers of Abyssinia and Ptolemaic Egypt were interfering in the Red Sea area and carrying their aggression into the Yemen proper. In the first quarter of the 6th century the proselytizing efforts of a Jewish Yemeni ruler resulted in a massacre of Christians in the major Christian centre of Najran. This event invited Abyssinian Christian reprisal and occupation, which put a virtual end to indigenous control of the Yemen. In conflict with the Byzantines, the Zoroastrian-Mazdean Sasanians invaded Yemen toward the end of the 6th century, further expanding the religious and cultural horizons of Arabia, where membership in a religious community could not be apolitical and could even have international ramifications. The connection between communal affiliation and political orientations would be expressed in the early Muslim community and in fact has continued to function to the present day.

The long-term result of Arabia's entry into international politics was paradoxical: it enhanced the power of the tribal Arabs at the expense of the "superpowers." Living in an ecological environment that favoured tribal independence and small-group loyalties, the Arabs had never established lasting large-scale states, only transient tribal confederations. By the 5th century, however, the settled powers needed their hinterlands enough to foster client states: the Byzantines oversaw the Ghassanid kingdom; the Persians oversaw the Lakhmid; and the Yemenis (prior to the Abyssinian invasion) had Kindah. These relationships increased Arab awareness of other cultures and religions, and the awareness seems to have stimulated internal Arab cultural activity, especially the classical Arabic, or *mudari*, poetry, for which the pre-Islamic Arabs are so famous. In the north, Arabic speakers were drawn into the imperial administrations of the Romans and Sasanians. Soon certain settled and semi-settled Arabs spoke and wrote Aramaic or Persian as well as Arabic, and some Persian or Aramaic speakers could speak and write Arabic. The prosperity of the 5th and 6th centuries, as well as the intensification of imperial rivalries in the late 6th century, seems to have brought the Arabs of the interior permanently into the wider network of communication that fostered the rise of the Muslim community at Mecca and Medina.

CHAPTER 2

FORMATION AND ORIENTATION (C. 500–634)

A critical period of formation and orientation between the emergence of the Islamic faith and the death of Abu Bakr (reigned 632–634), the first of the Rashidun (Arabic: "Rightly Guided") caliphs, centred first on the city of Mecca (Makkah) and swiftly unfolded toward Yathrib (later known as Medina) and beyond. Although strong bonds of faith within the nascent community of believers were accentuated by the experience of persecution in Mecca, it was only after the emigration of the community in 622 to Yathrib, that the Islamic community-state began to emerge in earnest.

THE CITY OF MECCA: CENTRE OF TRADE AND RELIGION

Although the 6th-century client states were the largest Arab polities of their day, it was not from them that a permanently significant Arab state arose. Rather, it emerged among independent Arabs living in Mecca at the junction of major north–south and west–east routes, in one of the less naturally favoured Arab settlements of the Hejaz (al-Hijaz). The development of a trading town into a city-state was not unusual, but, unlike many other western Arabian settlements, Mecca was not centred on an oasis or located in the hinterland of any non-Arab power. Although it had enough well water and springwater to provide for large numbers of camels, it did not have enough for agriculture; its economy depended on long-distance as well as short-distance trade.

MECCA UNDER THE QURAYSH CLANS

Sometime after the year 400 CE Mecca had come under the control of a group of Arabs who were in the process of becoming sedentary; they were known as Quraysh and were led by a man remembered as Qusayy ibn Kilab (called al-Mujammi', "the Unifier"). During the generations before Muhammad's birth in about 570, the several clans of the Quraysh fostered a development in Mecca that seems to have been occurring in a few other Arab towns as well. They used their trading connections and their relationships with their Bedouin cousins to make their town a regional centre whose influence radiated in many directions. They designated Mecca as a quarterly *haram*, a safe haven from the intertribal warfare and raiding that was endemic among the Bedouin. Thus, Mecca became an attractive site for large trade fairs that coincided with pilgrimage (Arabic: *hajj*) to a local shrine, the Ka'bah. The Ka'bah housed the deities of visitors as well as the Meccans' supra-tribal creator and covenant-guaranteeing deity, called Allah. Most Arabs probably viewed this deity as one among many,

This painting from the 16th century depicts Muhammad and his companions, attended by angels, as they approach Mecca. Topkapi Palace Museum, Istanbul, Turkey/ Bildarchiv Steffens/ The Bridgeman Art Library

possessing powers not specific to a particular tribe; others may have identified this figure with the God of the Jews and Christians.

The building activities of the Quraysh threatened one non-Arab power enough to invite direct interference: the Abyssinians are said to have invaded Mecca in the year of Muhammad's birth. But the Byzantines and Sasanians were distracted by internal reorganization and renewed conflict; simultaneously the Yemeni kingdoms were declining. Furthermore, these shifts in the international balance of power may have dislocated existing tribal connections enough to make Mecca an attractive new focus for supra-tribal organization, just as Mecca's equidistance from the major powers protected its independence and neutrality.

The Meccan link between shrine and market has a broader significance in the history of religion. It is reminiscent of changes that had taken place with the emergence of complex societies across the settled world several millennia earlier. Much of the religious life of the tribal Arabs had the characteristics of small-group, or "primitive," religion, including the sacralization of group-specific natural objects and phenomena and the multifarious presence of spirit beings, known among the Arabs as *jinn*. Where more-complex settlement patterns had developed, however, widely shared deities had already emerged, such as the "trinity" of Allah's "daughters" known as al-Lat, Manat, and al-'Uzza. Such qualified simplification and inclusivity, wherever they have occurred in human history, seem to have been associated with other fundamental changes — increased settlement, extension and intensification of trade, and the emergence of lingua francas and other cultural commonalties, all of which had been occurring in central Arabia for several centuries.

NEW SOCIAL PATTERNS AMONG THE MECCANS AND THEIR NEIGHBOURS

The sedentarization of the Quraysh and their efforts to create an expanding network of cooperative Arabs generated social stresses that demanded new patterns of behaviour. The ability of the Quraysh to solve their problems was affected by an ambiguous relationship between sedentary and migratory Arabs. Tribal Arabs could go in and out of sedentarization easily, and kinship ties often transcended lifestyles. The sedentarization of the Quraysh did not involve the destruction of their ties with the Bedouin or their idealization of Bedouin life. Thus, for example, did wealthy Meccans, thinking Mecca unhealthy, often send their infants to Bedouin foster mothers. Yet the settling of the Quraysh at Mecca was no ordinary instance of sedentarization. Their commercial success produced a society unlike that of the Bedouin and unlike that of many other sedentary Arabs. Whereas stratification was minimal among the Bedouin, a hierarchy based on wealth appeared among the Quraysh. Although a Bedouin group might include a small number of outsiders, such as prisoners of war, Meccan society was markedly diverse, including non-Arabs as well as Arabs, slave as well as free. Among the Bedouin, lines of protection for in-group members were clearly drawn; in Mecca, sedentarization and socioeconomic stratification had begun to blur family responsibilities and foster the growth of an oligarchy whose economic objectives could easily supersede other motivations and values. Whereas the Bedouin acted in and through groups and even regularized intergroup raiding and warfare as a way of life, Meccans needed to act in their own interest and to minimize conflict by institutionalizing new, broader social alliances and interrelationships.

The market-shrine complex encouraged surrounding tribes to put aside their conflicts periodically and to visit and worship the deities of the Ka'bah; but such worship, as in most complex societies, could not replace either the particularistic worship of small groups or the competing religious practices of other regional centres, such as al-Ta'if.

Very little in the Arabian environment favoured the formation of stable large-scale states. Therefore, Meccan efforts at centralization and unification might well have been transient, especially because they were not reinforced by any stronger power and because they depended almost entirely on the prosperity of a trade route that had been formerly controlled at its southern terminus and could be controlled elsewhere in the future, or exclude Mecca entirely. The rise of the Meccan system also coincided with the spread of the confessional religions, through immigration, missionization, conversion, and foreign interference. Alongside members of the confessional religions were unaffiliated monotheists, known as *hanifs*, who distanced themselves from the Meccan religious system by repudiating the old gods but embracing neither Judaism nor Christianity. Eventually in Mecca and elsewhere a few individuals came to envision the possibility of effecting supra-tribal association through a leadership role common to the confessional religions, that is, prophethood or messengership. The only such individual who succeeded in effecting broad social changes was a member of the Hashim (Hashem) clan of Quraysh named Muhammad ibn 'Abd Allah ibn 'Abd al-Muttalib. One of their own, he accomplished what the Quraysh had started, first by working against them, later by working with them. When he was born, around 570, the potential for pan-Arab unification seemed nil, but after he died, in 632, the first generation of his followers were able not only to maintain pan-Arab unification but also to expand far beyond the peninsula.

THE PROPHET MUHAMMAD

MUHAMMAD'S YEARS IN MECCA

SPIRITUAL AWAKENING

Any explanation of such an unprecedented development must include an analysis not only of Muhammad's individual genius but also of his ability to articulate an ideology capable of appealing to multiple constituencies. His approach to the role of prophet allowed a variety of groups to conceptualize and form a single community. Muhammad was, according to many students of social behaviour, particularly well placed to lead such a social movement; in both ascribed and acquired characteristics he was unusual. Although he was a member of a high-status tribe, he belonged to one of its less well-placed clans. He was fatherless at birth; his mother and grandfather died when he was young, leaving him under the protection of an uncle. Although he possessed certain admirable personality traits to an unusual degree, his commercial success derived not from his own status but from his marriage to a much older woman, a wealthy widow named Khadijah. During the years of his marriage, his personal habits grew increasingly atypical. He began to absent himself in the hills outside Mecca to engage in the solitary spiritual activity of the *hanif*s. At age 40, while on retreat, he saw a figure, whom he later identified as the angel Gabriel, who asked him to "recite" (*iqra'*), then overwhelmed him with a very strong embrace. Muhammad told the stranger that he was not a reciter. But the angel repeated his demand and embrace three times before the verses of the Qur'an, beginning with "Recite in the Name of thy Lord, who created," were revealed. Although a few individuals, including his wife Khadijah, recognized his experience as that of a messenger of God, the contemporary religious life of most of the Meccans and the surrounding Arabs did not prepare them to share in this recognition easily.

Arabs did recognize several other types of intermediaries with the sacred. Some of the kings of the Yemen are said to have had priestly functions. Tribal leaders, sheikhs, in protecting their tribes' hallowed custom (Sunnah), had a spiritual dimension. Tribal Arabs also had their *kahin*s, religious specialists who delivered oracles in ecstatic rhymed prose (*saj'*) and read omens. And they also had their *sha'ir*s, professionally trained oral poets who defended the group's honour, expressed its identity, and engaged in verbal duels with the poets of other groups. The power of the recited word was well established; the poets' words were even likened to arrows that could wound the unprotected enemy. Because Muhammad's utterances seemed similar, at least in form, to those of the *kahin*s, many of his hearers naturally assumed that he was one of the figures with whom they were more familiar. Indeed, Muhammad might not even have attracted attention had he not sounded like other holy men. But, by eschewing any source other than the one supreme being, whom he identified as Allah ("God") and whose message he regarded as cosmically significant and binding, he was gradually able to distinguish himself from all other intermediaries. Like many successful leaders, Muhammad broke through existing restraints by what might be called transformative conservatism. By combining familiar leadership roles with a less familiar one, he expanded his authority; by giving existing practices a new history, he reoriented them; by assigning a new cause to existing problems, he resolved them. His personal characteristics fit his historical circumstances perfectly.

PUBLIC RECITATIONS

Muhammad's first vision was followed by a brief lull, after which he began to hear messages frequently, entering a special physical state to receive them and returning to normalcy to deliver them orally. Soon he began publicly to recite warnings of an imminent reckoning by Allah that disturbed the Meccan leaders. Muhammad was one of their own, a man respected for his personal qualities. Yet weakening kinship ties and increasing social diversity were helping him attract followers from many different clans and also from among tribeless persons, giving all of them a new and potentially disruptive affiliation. The fundamentals of his message, delivered often in the vicinity of the Ka'bah itself, questioned the very reasons for which so many people gathered there. If visitors to the Ka'bah assumed, as so many Arabs did, that the deities represented by its idols were all useful and accessible in that place, Muhammad spoke, as had Axial Age figures before, of a placeless and timeless deity that not only had created human beings, making them dependent on him, but would also bring them to account at an apocalypse of his own making. In place of time or chance, which the Arabs assumed to govern their destiny, Muhammad installed a final reward or punishment based on individual actions. Such individual accountability to an unseen power that took no account whatsoever of kin relationships and operated beyond the Meccan system could, if taken seriously, undermine any authority the Quraysh had acquired. Muhammad's insistence on the protection of the weak, which echoed Bedouin values, threatened the unbridled amassing of wealth so important to the Meccan oligarchy.

EFFORTS TO REFORM MECCAN SOCIETY

Yet Muhammad also appealed to the town dweller by describing the human being as a member of a polis (city-state) and by suggesting ways to overcome the inequities that such an environment breeds. By insisting that an event of cosmic significance was occurring in Mecca, he made the town the rival of all the greater cities with which the Meccans traded. To Meccans who believed that what went on in their town and at their shrine was hallowed by tribal custom, Sunnah, Muhammad replied that their activities in fact were a corrupt form of a practice that had a very long history with the God of whom he spoke. In Muhammad's view, the Ka'bah had been dedicated to the aniconic worship of the one God (Allah) by Abraham, who fathered the ancestor of the Israelites, Ishaq (Isaac), as well as the ancestor of the Arabs, Isma'il (Ishmael). Muhammad asked his hearers not to embrace something new but to abandon the traditional in favour of the original. He appealed to his fellow Quraysh not to reject the Sunnah of their ancestors but rather to appreciate and fulfill its true nature. God should be worshipped not through offerings but through prayer and recitation of his messages, and his house should be emptied of its useless idols.

In their initial rejection of his appeal, Muhammad's Meccan opponents took the first step toward accepting the new idea: they attacked it. For it was their rejection of him, as well as his subsequent rejection by many Jews and Christians, that helped to forge Muhammad's followers into a community with an identity of its own and capable of ultimately incorporating its opponents. Muhammad's disparate following was exceptionally vulnerable, bound together not by kinship ties but by a "generic" monotheism that involved being faithful (*mu'min*) to the message

God was sending through their leader. Their vulnerability was mitigated by the absence of formal municipal discipline, but their opponents within the Quraysh could apply informal pressures ranging from harassment and violence against the weakest to a boycott against Muhammad's clan, members of which were persuaded by his uncle Abu Talib to remain loyal even though most of them were not his followers. Meanwhile, Muhammad and his closest associates were thinking about reconstituting themselves as a separate community in a less hostile environment. In about 615, some 80 of his followers made an emigration (Hijrah) to Abyssinia, perhaps assuming that they would be welcome in a place that had a history of hostility to the Meccan oligarchy and that worshipped the same God who had sent Muhammad to them, but they eventually returned without establishing a permanent community. During the next decade, continued rejection intensified the group's identity and its search for another home. Although the boycott against Muhammad's clan began to disintegrate, the deaths of his wife and his uncle, about 619, removed an important source of psychological and social support. Muhammad had already begun to preach and attract followers at market gatherings outside Mecca; now he intensified his search for a more hospitable environment. In 620, he met with a delegation of followers from Yathrib, an oasis about 200 miles (320 km) to the northeast. In the next two years their support grew into an offer of protection.

MUHAMMAD'S EMIGRATION TO YATHRIB (MEDINA)

Like Mecca, Yathrib was experiencing demographic problems: several tribal groups coexisted, descendants of its Arab Jewish founders as well as a number of pagan Arab immigrants divided into two tribes, the Aws and the

Khazraj. Unable to resolve their conflicts, the Yathribis invited Muhammad to perform the well-established role of neutral outside arbiter (*hakam*). In September 622, having discreetly sent his followers ahead, he and one companion, Abu Bakr, completed the community's second and final emigration, barely avoiding Quraysh attempts to prevent his departure by force. By the time of the emigration, a new label had begun to appear in Muhammad's recitations to describe his followers: in addition to being described in terms of their faithfulness (*iman*) to God and his messenger, they were also described in terms of their undivided attention—that is, as *muslim*s, individuals who assumed the right relationship to God by surrendering (*islam*) to his will. Although the designation *muslim*, derived from *islam*, eventually became a proper name for a specific historical community, at this point it appears to have expressed commonality with other monotheists. Like the others, *muslim*s faced Jerusalem to pray; Muhammad was believed to have been transported from Jerusalem to the heavens to talk with God; and Abraham, Noah, Moses, David, and Jesus, as well as Muhammad, all were considered to be prophets (*nabi*s) and messengers of the same God. In Yathrib, however, conflicts between other monotheists and the *muslim*s sharpened their distinctiveness.

THE FORGING OF MUHAMMAD'S COMMUNITY

As an autonomous community, *muslim*s might have become a tribal unit like those with whom they had affiliated, especially because the terms of their immigration gave them no special status. Yet under Muhammad's leadership they developed a social organization that could absorb or challenge everyone around them. They became Muhammad's *ummah* ("community") because they had recognized and supported God's emissary (*rasul Allah*). The *ummah*'s

The Prophet's Mosque, where he is buried in Medina, Saudi Arabia. This mosque is the second holiest site in Islam. Awad Awad/AFP/Getty Images

members differed from one another not by wealth or genealogical superiority but by the degree of their faith and piety, and membership in the community was itself an expression of faith. Anyone could join, regardless of origin, by following Muhammad's lead, and the nature of members' support could vary. In the concept of *ummah*, Muhammad supplied the missing ingredient in the Meccan system: a powerful abstract principle for defining, justifying, and stimulating membership in a single community.

Muhammad made the concept of *ummah* work by expanding his role as arbiter so as to become the sole spokesman for all residents of Yathrib, hereafter called

Medina. Even though the agreement under which Muhammad had emigrated did not obligate non-Muslims to follow him except in his arbitration, they necessarily became involved in the fortunes of his community. By protecting him from his Meccan enemies, the residents of Medina identified with his fate. Those who supported him as Muslims received special designations: the Medinans were called *ansar* ("helpers"), and his fellow emigrants were distinguished as *muhajirun* ("emigrants"). He was often able to use revelation to arbitrate.

Because the terms of his emigration did not provide adequate financial support, he began to provide for his community through caravan raiding, a tactic familiar to tribal Arabs. By thus inviting hostility, he required all the Medinans to take sides. Initial failure was followed by success, first at Nakhlah, where the Muslims defied Meccan custom by violating one of the truce months so essential to Meccan prosperity and prestige. Their most memorable victory occurred in 624 at Badr, against a large Meccan force; they continued to succeed, with only one serious setback, at Uhud in 625. From that time on, "conversion" to Islam involved joining an established polity, the successes of which were tied to its proper spiritual orientation, regardless of whether the convert shared that orientation completely. During the early years in Medina a major motif of Islamic history emerged: the connection between material success and divine favour, which had also been prominent in the history of the Israelites.

THE *UMMAH*'S ALLIES AND ENEMIES

During these years, Muhammad used his outstanding knowledge of tribal relations to act as a great tribal leader, or sheikh, further expanding his authority beyond the role that the Medinans had given him. He developed a network

BATTLE OF BADR

The early military victory of the Prophet Muhammad at the Battle of Badr (624 CE) seriously damaged Meccan prestige while strengthening the political position of Muslims in Medina and establishing Islam as a viable force in the Arabian Peninsula.

Since their emigration from Mecca (622), the Muslims in Medina had depended for economic survival on constant raids on Meccan caravans. When word of a particularly wealthy caravan escorted by Abu Sufyan, head of the Umayyad clan, reached Muhammad, a raiding party of about 300 Muslims, to be led by Muhammad himself, was organized. By filling the wells on the caravan route near Medina with sand, the Muslims lured Abu Sufyan's army to battle at Badr, near Medina, in March 624. Despite the superior numbers of the Meccan forces (about 1,000 men), the Muslims scored a complete victory, and many prominent Meccans were killed. The success at Badr was recorded in the Qur'an as a divine sanction of the new religion: "It was not you who slew them, it was God . . . in order that He might test the Believers by a gracious trial from Himself" (8:17). Those Muslims who fought at Badr became known as the *badriyun* and make up one group of the Companions of the Prophet.

of alliances between his *ummah* and neighbouring tribes, and so competed with the Meccans at their own game. He managed and distributed the booty from raiding, keeping one-fifth for the *ummah*'s overall needs and distributing the rest among its members. In return, members gave a portion of their wealth as *zakat*, a tax paid to help the needy and to demonstrate their awareness of their dependence on God for all of their material benefits. Like other sheikhs, Muhammad contracted numerous, often strategically motivated, marriage alliances. He was also more able to harass and discipline Medinans, Muslim and non-Muslim alike, who did not support his activities fully. He agitated in particular against the Jews, one of whose clans, the Banu Qaynuqa', he expelled.

Increasingly estranged from nonresponsive Jews and Christians, he reoriented his followers' direction of prayer from Jerusalem to Mecca. He formally instituted the *hajj* to Mecca and fasting during the month of Ramadan as distinctive cultic acts, in recognition of the fact that *islam*, a generic act of surrender to God, had become Islam, a proper-name identity distinguished not only from paganism but from other forms of monotheism as well. As more and more of Medina was absorbed into the Muslim community and as the Meccans weakened, Muhammad's authority expanded. He continued to lead a three-pronged campaign — against nonsupporters in Medina, against the Quraysh in Mecca, and against surrounding tribes — and he even ordered raids into southern Syria. Eventually Muhammad became powerful enough to punish nonsupporters severely, especially those who leaned toward Mecca. For example, he had the men of the Qurayzah clan of Jews in Medina executed after they failed to help him against the Meccan forces at the Battle of the Ditch in 627. But he also used force and diplomacy to bring in other Jewish and Christian groups. Because they were seen, unlike pagans, to have formed *ummah*s of their own around a revelation from God, Jews and Christians were entitled to pay for protection (*dhimmah*). Muhammad thus set a precedent for another major characteristic of Islamicate civilization, that of qualified religious pluralism under Muslim authority.

MUHAMMAD'S LATER RECITATIONS

During these years of warfare and consolidation, Muhammad continued to transmit revealed recitations, though their nature began to change. Some commented

BATTLE OF THE DITCH

Victory at the Battle of the Ditch (Arabic: *Al-Khandaq* ["The Ditch"]) in 627 CE ultimately forced the Meccans to recognize the political and religious strength of the Muslim community in Medina.

A Meccan army of 3,000 men had defeated the undisciplined Muslim forces at Uhud near Medina in 625, wounding Muhammad himself. In March 627, when they had persuaded a number of Bedouin tribes to join their cause, the Meccans brought a force of 10,000 men against Medina again. Muhammad then resorted to tactics unfamiliar to the Arabs, who were accustomed to brief, isolated raids. Rather than sally out to meet the enemy in the usual way—the mistake made at Uhud—he had a ditch dug around Medina, according to tradition, at the suggestion of a Persian convert, Salman. The Meccan horsemen were disconcerted and soon grew bored of the siege, and the coalition of Bedouin tribes started breaking up. After an unsuccessful siege, the Meccans dispersed. With the Muslim and Meccan forces now more evenly matched and the Meccans tiring of a war that was damaging their trade, Muhammad used his victory to negotiate greater concessions for the Muslims in a treaty at al-Hudaybiyah (628).

on Muhammad's situation, consoled and encouraged his community, explained the continuing resistance of the Meccans, and urged appropriate responses. Some told stories about figures familiar to Jews and Christians but cast in an Islamic framework. Though still delivered in the form of God's direct speech, the messages became longer and less ecstatic, less urgent in their warnings if more earnest in their guidance. Eventually they focused on interpersonal regulations in areas of particular importance for a new community, such as sexuality, marriage, divorce, and inheritance. By this time certain Muslims had begun to write down what Muhammad uttered or to recite passages for worship (*salat*) and private devotion. The recited word, so important among the Arab tribes, had found a greatly enlarged significance. A competitor for Muhammad's status as God's messenger even declared himself among a nonmember tribe; he was Musaylimah of Yamamah, who claimed to convey revelations from God. He managed to attract numerous Bedouin Arabs but failed to speak as successfully as Muhammad to the various available constituencies.

Activism in the name of God, both nonmilitary as well as military, would become a permanent strand in Muslim piety. Given the environment in which Muhammad operated, his *ummah* was unlikely to survive without it; to compete as leader of a community, he needed to exhibit military prowess. (Like most successful leaders, however, Muhammad was a moderate and a compromiser; some of his followers were more militant and aggressive than he, and some were less so.) In addition, circumstantial necessity had ideological ramifications. Because Muhammad as messenger was also, by divine providence, leader of an established community, he could easily define the whole realm of social action as an expression of faith. Thus, Muslims were able to identify messengership with worldly leadership to an extent almost unparalleled in the history of religion. There had been activist prophets before Muhammad and there were activist prophets after him, but in no other religious tradition does the image of the activist prophet, and by extension the activist follower, have such a comprehensive and coherent justification in the formative period.

ISLAM AT MUHAMMAD'S DEATH

Muhammad's continuing success gradually impinged on the Quraysh in Mecca. Some defected and joined his community. His marriage to a Quraysh woman provided him with a useful go-between. In 628 he and his followers tried to make an Islamized *hajj* but were forestalled by the Meccans. At Al-Hudaybiyah, outside Mecca, Muhammad granted a 10-year truce on the condition that the Meccans would allow a Muslim pilgrimage the next year. Even at this point, however, Muhammad's control over his followers had its limits; his more zealous followers agreed to the pact only after much persuasion. As in all instances of charismatic leadership, persisting loyalty was correlated with continuing success. In the next year the Meccans allowed a Muslim *hajj*; and in the next year, 630, the Muslims occupied Mecca without a struggle. Muhammad began to receive deputations from many parts of Arabia. By his death in 632 he was ruler of virtually all of it.

The Meccan Quraysh were allowed to become Muslims without shame. In fact, they quickly became assimilated to the actual *muhajirun*, even though they had not emigrated to Medina themselves. Ironically, in defeat they had accomplished much more than they would have had they achieved victory: the centralization of all of Arabia around their polity and their shrine, the Ka'bah, which had been emptied of its idols to be filled with an infinitely greater invisible power.

Because intergroup conflict was banned to all members of the *ummah* on the basis of their shared loyalty to the emissary of a single higher authority, the limitations of the Meccan concept of *haram*, according to which the city quarterly became a safe haven, could be overcome. The broader solidarity that Muhammad had begun to build was stabilized only after his death, and this was achieved, paradoxically, by some of the same people who had initially opposed him. In the next two years one of his most significant legacies became apparent: the willingness and ability of his closest supporters to sustain the ideal and the reality of one Muslim community under one leader, even in the face of significant opposition. When Muhammad died, two vital sources of his authority ended—ongoing revelation and his unique ability to exemplify his messages on a daily basis. A leader capable of keeping revelation alive might have had the best chance of inheriting his movement, but no Muslim claimed messengership, nor had Muhammad unequivocally designated any other type of successor. The *ansar*, his early supporters in Medina, moved to elect their own leader, leaving the *muhajirun* to choose theirs, but a small number of *muhajirun* managed to impose one of their own over the whole. That man was Abu Bakr, one of Muhammad's earliest followers and the father of his favourite wife, 'A'ishah. The title Abu Bakr took, *khalifah* (caliph), meaning deputy or successor, echoed revealed references to those who assist major leaders and even God himself. To *khalifah* he appended *rasul Allah*, so that his authority was based on his assistance to Muhammad as messenger of God.

ABU BAKR'S SUCCESSION

Abu Bakr soon confronted two new threats: the secession of many of the tribes that had joined the *ummah* after 630 and the appearance among them of other prophet figures who claimed continuing guidance from God. In withdrawing, the tribes appear to have been able to distinguish loyalty to Muhammad from full acceptance of the uniqueness and permanence of his message. The appearance of other prophets illustrates a general phenomenon in the history of religion: the volatility of revelation as a source of authority. When successfully claimed, it has almost no competitor; once opened, it is difficult to close; and, if it cannot be contained and focused at the appropriate moment, its power disperses. Jews and Christians had

RIDDAH

The *riddah* wars, or wars of apostasy, were a series of politico-religious uprisings in various parts of Arabia in about 632 CE during the caliphate of Abu Bakr.

In spite of the traditional resistance of the Bedouins to any restraining central authority, by 631 Muhammad was able to exact from the majority of their tribes at least nominal adherence to Islam, payment of the *zakat*, a tax levied on Muslims to support the poor, and acceptance of Medinan envoys. In March 632, in what Muslim historians later called the first apostasy, or *riddah*, a Yemeni tribe expelled two of Muhammad's agents and secured control of Yemen. Muhammad died three months later, and dissident tribes, eager to reassert their independence and stop payment of the *zakat*, rose in revolt. They refused to recognize the authority of Abu Bakr, interpreting Muhammad's death as a termination of their contract, and rallied instead around at least four rival prophets.

Most of Abu Bakr's reign was consequently occupied with *riddah* wars, which under the generalship of Khalid ibn al-Walid not only brought the secessionists back to Islam but also won over many who had not yet been converted. The major campaign was directed against Abu Bakr's strongest opponent, the prophet Musaylimah and his followers in Al-Yamamah. It culminated in a notoriously bloody battle at 'Aqraba' in eastern Najd (May 633), afterward known as the Garden of Death. The encounter cost the Muslims the lives of many *ansar* ("helpers"; Medinan Companions of the Prophet) who were invaluable for their knowledge of the Qur'an, which had been revealed to the Prophet, recited to his disciples, and memorized by them but not yet written down. Musaylimah was killed, the heart of the *riddah* opposition was destroyed, and the strength of the Medinan government was established. Sometime between 633 and 634 Arabia was finally reunited under the caliph, and the energy of its tribes was diverted to the conquest of Iraq, Syria, and Egypt.

responded to this dilemma in their own ways; now it was the turn of the Muslims, whose future was dramatically affected by Abu Bakr's response. He put an end to revelation with a combination of military force and coherent rhetoric. He defined withdrawal from Muhammad's coalition as ingratitude to or denial of God (the concept of *kufr*. Thus he gave secession (*riddah*) cosmic significance as an act of apostasy punishable, according to God's revealed messages to Muhammad, by death. He declared that the secessionists had become Muslims, and thus servants of God, by joining Muhammad. They were not free not to be Muslims, nor could they be Muslims, and thus loyal to God, under any leader whose legitimacy did not derive from Muhammad. Finally, he declared Muhammad to be the last prophet God would send, relying on a reference to Muhammad in one of the revealed messages as *khatm al-anbiya'* ("seal of the prophets"). In his ability to interpret the events of his reign from the perspective of Islam, Abu Bakr demonstrated the power of the new conceptual vocabulary Muhammad had introduced.

Had Abu Bakr not asserted the independence and uniqueness of Islam, the movement he had inherited could have been splintered or absorbed by other monotheistic communities or by new Islam-like movements led by other tribal figures. Moreover, had he not quickly made the ban on secession and intergroup conflict yield material success, his chances for survival would have been very slim, because Arabia's resources could not support his state. To provide an adequate fiscal base, Abu Bakr enlarged impulses present in pre-Islamic Mecca and in the *ummah*. At his death he was beginning to turn his followers to raiding non-Muslims in the only direction where that was possible, the north. Migration into Syria and Iraq already had a long history; Arabs, both migratory and settled, were already present there. Indeed, some of them were already launching raids when 'Umar I, Abu Bakr's acknowledged successor, assumed the caliphate in 634. The ability of the Medinan state to absorb random action into a relatively centralized movement of expansion testifies to the strength of the new ideological and administrative patterns inherent in the concept of *ummah*.

The fusion of two once separable phenomena, membership in Muhammad's community and faith in Islam—the mundane and the spiritual—would become one of Islam's most distinctive features. Becoming and being Muslim always involved doing more than it involved believing. On balance, Muslims have always favoured orthopraxy (correctness of practice) over orthodoxy (correctness of doctrine). Being Muslim has always meant making a commitment to a set of behavioral patterns because they reflect the right orientation to God. Where choices were later posed, they were posed not in terms of religion and politics, or church and state, but between living in the world the right way or the wrong way. Just as classical Islamicate languages developed no equivalents for the words *religion* and *politics*, modern European languages have developed no adequate terms to capture the choices as Muslims have posed them.

CHAPTER 3

CONVERSION AND CRYSTALLIZATION (634–870)

The Arab conquests are often viewed as a discrete period. The end of the conquests appears to be a convenient dividing line because it coincides with a conventional watershed, the overthrow of the Umayyad caliphs by the 'Abbasids. To illustrate their role in broader social and cultural change, however, the military conquests should be included in a period more than twice as long, during which the conquest of the hearts and minds of the majority of the subject population also occurred. Between 634 and 870 Islam was transformed from the badge of a small Arab ruling class to the dominant faith of a vast empire that stretched from the western Mediterranean into Central Asia.

SOCIAL AND CULTURAL TRANSFORMATIONS

As a result of so long and gradual a period of conversion, Arab cultures intermingled with the indigenous cultures of the conquered peoples to produce Islam's fundamental orientations and identities. The Arabic language became a vehicle for the transmission of high culture, even though the Arabs remained a minority. For the first time in the history of the Nile-to-Oxus region, a new language of high culture, carrying a great cultural florescence, replaced all previous languages of high culture. Trade and taxation replaced booty as the fiscal basis of the Muslim state; a nontribal army replaced a tribal one; and a centralized empire became a nominal confederation, with all of the social dislocation and rivalries those changes imply.

Yet despite continuous internal dissension, virtually no Muslim raised the possibility of there being more than one legitimate leader. Furthermore, the impulse toward solidarity, inherited from Muhammad and Abu Bakr, may have actually been encouraged by persisting minority status. While Muslims were a minority, they naturally formed a conception of Islamic dominance as territorial rather than religious, and of unconverted non-Muslim communities as secondary members. In one important respect the Islamic faith differed from all other major religious traditions: the formative period of the faith coincided with its political domination of a rich complex of old cultures. As a result, during the formative period of their civilization, the Muslims could both introduce new elements and reorient old ones in creative ways.

Just as Muhammad fulfilled and redirected ongoing tendencies in Arabia, the builders of early Islamicate civilization carried forth and transformed developments in the Roman and Sasanian territories in which they first dominated. While Muhammad was emerging as a leader in the Hejaz, the Byzantine and Sasanian emperors were ruling states that resembled what the Islamicate empire was to become. Byzantine rule stretched from North

Africa into Syria and sometimes Iraq; the Sasanians competed with the Byzantines in Syria and Iraq and extended their sway, at its furthest, across the Oxus River. Among their subjects were speakers and writers of several major languages—various forms of Aramaic, such as Mandaean and Syriac; Greek; Arabic; and Middle Persian. In fact, a significant number of persons were probably bilingual or trilingual. Both the Byzantine and the Sasanian empire declared an official religion, Christianity and Zoroastrian-Mazdeism, respectively. The Sasanian empire in the early 7th century was ruled by a religion-backed centralized monarchy with an elaborate bureaucratic structure that was reproduced on a smaller scale at the provincial courts of its appointed governors. Its religious demography was complex, encompassing Christians of many persuasions, including monophysites, Nestorians, Orthodox, and others; pagans; gnostics; Jews; and Mazdeans. Minority religious communities were becoming more clearly organized and isolated. The population included priests; traders and merchants; landlords (*dihqans*), sometimes living not on the land but as absentees in the cities; pastoralists; and large numbers of peasant agriculturalists. In southern Iraq, especially in and around towns like Al-Hirah, it included migratory and settled Arabs as well. Both empires relied on standing armies for their defense and on agriculture, taxation, conquest, and trade for their resources. When the Muslim conquests began, the Byzantines and Sasanians had been in conflict for a century; in the most recent exchanges, the Sasanians had established direct rule in al-Hirah, further exposing its many Arabs to their administration. When the Arab conquests began, representatives of Byzantine and Sasanian rule on Arabia's northern borders were not strong enough to resist.

'UMAR I'S SUCCESSION

THE SPIRIT OF CONQUEST UNDER 'UMAR I

Abu Bakr's successor in Medina, 'Umar I (ruled 634–644), had not so much to stimulate conquest as he had to organize and channel it. He chose as leaders skillful managers experienced in trade and commerce as well as warfare and imbued with an ideology that provided their activities with a cosmic significance. The total numbers involved in the initial conquests may have been relatively small, perhaps less than 50,000, divided into numerous shifting groups. Yet few actions took place without any sanction from the Medinan government or one of its appointed commanders. The fighters, or *muqatilah*, could generally accomplish much more with Medina's support than without. 'Umar, one of Muhammad's earliest and staunchest supporters, had quickly developed an administrative system of manifestly superior effectiveness. He defined the *ummah* as a continually expansive polity managed by a new ruling elite, which included successful military commanders like Khalid ibn al-Walid. Even after the conquests ended, this sense of expansiveness continued to be expressed in the way Muslims divided the world into their own zone, the Dar al-Islam, and the zone into which they could and should expand, the Dar al-Harb, the abode of war. The norms of 'Umar's new elite were supplied by Islam as it was then understood. Taken together, Muhammad's revelations from God and his Sunnah (precedent-setting example) defined the cultic and personal practices that distinguished Muslims from others: prayer, fasting, pilgrimage, charity, avoidance of pork and intoxicants, membership in one community centred at Mecca, and activism (jihad) on the community's behalf.

FORGING THE LINK OF ACTIVISM WITH FAITHFULNESS

'Umar symbolized this conception of the *ummah* in two ways. He assumed an additional title, *amir al-mu'minin* ("commander of the faithful"), which linked organized activism with faithfulness (*iman*), the earliest defining feature of the Muslim. He also adopted a lunar calendar that began with the emigration (Hijrah), the moment at which a group of individual followers of Muhammad had become an active social presence. Because booty was the *ummah*'s major resource, 'Umar concentrated on ways to distribute and sustain it. He established a *diwan*, or register, to pay all members of the ruling elite and the conquering forces, from Muhammad's family on down, in order of

The Umayyad Mosque, located in Damascus, Syria, holds a shrine said to contain the head of John the Baptist. DEA/G. Dagli Orti/Getty Images

entry into the *ummah*. The immovable booty was kept for the state. After the government's fifth-share of the movable booty was reserved, the rest was distributed according to the *diwan*. The *muqatilah* he stationed as an occupying army in garrisons (*amsar*) constructed in locations strategic to further conquest: al-Fustat in Egypt, Damascus in Syria, Kufah and Basra in Iraq. The garrisons attracted indigenous population and initiated significant demographic changes, such as a population shift from northern to southern Iraq. They also inaugurated the rudiments of an "Islamic" daily life; each garrison was commanded by a caliphal appointee, responsible for setting aside an area for prayer, a mosque (*masjid*), named for the prostrations (*sujud*) that had become a characteristic element in the five daily worship sessions (*salat*s). There the fighters could hear God's revelations to Muhammad recited by men trained in that emerging art. The most pious might commit the whole work to memory. There too, the Friday midday *salat* could be performed communally, accompanied by an important educational device, the sermon (*khutbah*), through which the fighters could be instructed in the principles of the faith. The mosque fused the practical and the spiritual in a special way: because the Friday prayer included an expression of loyalty to the ruler, it could also provide an opportunity to declare rebellion.

The series of ongoing conquests that fueled this system had their most extensive phase under 'Umar and his successor 'Uthman ibn 'Affan (ruled 644–656). Within 25 years Muslim Arab forces created the first empire to permanently link western Asia with the Mediterranean. Within another century Muslim conquerors surpassed the achievement of Alexander the Great, not only in the durability of their accomplishment but in its scope as well, reaching from the Iberian Peninsula to Central Asia. Resistance was generally slight and nondestructive, and conquest through capitulation was preferred to conquest by force. After the Sasanian city of Al-Hirah fell in 633, a large Byzantine force was defeated in Syria, opening the way to the final conquest of Damascus in 636. The next year further gains were made in Sasanian territory, especially at the Battle of al-Qadisiyyah, and in the next the focus returned to Syria and the taking of Jerusalem. By 640 Roman control in Syria was over, and by 641 the Sasanians had lost all their territory west of the Zagros. During the years 642 to 646 Egypt was taken under the leadership of 'Amr ibn al-'As, who soon began raids into what the Muslims called the Maghrib, the lands west of Egypt. Shortly thereafter, in the east, Persepolis fell; in 651 the defeat and assassination of the last Sasanian emperor, Yazdegerd III, marked the end of the 400-year-old Sasanian empire.

'UTHMAN'S SUCCESSION AND POLICIES

DISCONTENT IN 'UTHMAN'S REIGN

This phase of conquest ended under 'Uthman and ramified widely. 'Uthman may even have sent an emissary to China in 651; by the end of the 7th century Arab Muslims were trading there. The fiscal strain of such expansion and the growing independence of local Arabs outside the peninsula underlay the persisting discontents that surfaced toward the end of 'Uthman's reign. The very way in which he was made caliph had already signaled the potential for competition over leadership and resources. Perceived as pliable and docile, he was the choice of the small committee charged by the dying 'Umar with selecting one of their own number. Once in office, however, 'Uthman acted to establish the power of Medina over and against some of the powerful Quraysh families at Mecca and local notables outside Arabia. He was accused of nepotism for relying on his own family, the Banu Umayyah, whose talents 'Umar had already recognized. Among his many other "objectionable" acts was his call for the production of a single standard collection of Muhammad's messages from God, which was known simply as the Qur'an ("Recitation" or "Recitations"). Simultaneously he ordered the destruction of any other collections. Although they might have differed only in minor respects, they represented the independence of local communities. Above all, 'Uthman was the natural target of anyone dissatisfied with the distribution of the conquest's wealth, since he represented and defended a system that defined all income as Medina's to distribute.

The difficulties of 'Uthman's reign took more than a century to resolve. They were the inevitable result not just of the actions of individuals but of the whole process initiated by Muhammad's achievements. His coalition had been fragile. He had disturbed existing social arrangements without being able to reconstruct and stabilize new ones quickly. Into a society organized along family lines, he had introduced the supremacy of trans-kinship ties. Yet he had been forced to make use of kinship ties himself; and, despite his egalitarian message, he had introduced new inequities by granting privileges to the earliest and most intensely devoted followers of his cause. Furthermore, personal rivalries were stimulated by his charisma; individuals like his wife 'A'ishah, his daughter Fatimah, and her husband 'Ali frequently vied for his affection. 'Umar's *diwan* had, then, reinforced old inequities by extending privileges to wealthy high-placed Meccans, and it had introduced new tensions by assigning a lower status to those, indigenous or immigrant to the provinces, who joined the cause later (but who felt themselves to be making an equivalent or greater contribution). Other tensions resulted from conditions in the conquered lands: the initial isolation of Arab Muslims, and even Arab Christians who fought with them, from the indigenous non-Arab population; the discouragement of non-Arab converts, except as clients (*mawali*) of Arab tribes; the administrative dependence of peninsular Arabs on local Arabs and non-Arabs; and the development of a tax system that discriminated against non-Muslims.

INTRA-MUSLIM CONFLICTS

The ensuing conflicts were played out in a series of intra-Muslim disputes that began with 'Uthman's assassination in 656 and continued to the end of the period under discussion. The importance of kinship ties persisted, but they were gradually replaced by the identities of a new social order. These new identities resulted from Muslim responses to anti-Muslim activity as well as from Muslim participation in a series of controversies focused on the issue of leadership. Because the *ummah*, unified under one leader, was seen as an earthly expression of God's favour, and because God was seen as the controller of all aspects of human existence, the identities formed in the course of the *ummah*'s early history could fuse dimensions that secular modern observers are able to distinguish—religious, social, political, and economic. Furthermore, intra-Muslim rivalries changed during the conversion period; the meaningfulness of the new identities expanded as non-Muslims contributed to Islam's formation, through opposition or through conversion, and the key issues broadened as the participating constituencies enlarged. At first the disputes were coterminous with intra-Arab, indeed even intra-Quraysh, rivalries; only later did they involve persons of other backgrounds. Thus the faith of Islam was formed in conjunction with the crises that attended the establishment of rule by Muslims. Muslims might have produced an extremely localized and exclusivistic religion; but in spite of, and perhaps because of, their willingness to engage in continuing internal conflicts, they produced one of the most unified religious traditions in human history.

THE FOUR *FITNAHS*

By the end of the period of conversion and crystallization, Muslim historians would retrospectively identify four discrete periods of conflict and label them *fitnah*s, trials or temptations to test the unity of the *ummah*. Many historians also came to view some identities formed during the *fitnah*s as authentic and others as deviant. This retrospective interpretation may be anachronistic and misleading. The entire period between 656 and the last quarter of the 9th century was conflict-ridden, and the *fitnah*s merely mark periods of intensification; yet the most striking characteristic of the period was the pursuit of unity.

THE FIRST *FITNAH*

In the first two *fitnah*s the claimants to the caliphate relied on their high standing among the Quraysh and their local support in either Arabia, Iraq, or Syria. Competition for the caliphate thus reflected rivalries among the leading Arab families as well as regional interests. The first *fitnah* occurred between 'Uthman's assassination in 656 and the accession of his kinsman Mu'awiyah I in 661 and included the caliphate of 'Ali, the cousin and son-in-law of Muhammad. It involved a three-way contest between 'Ali's

An Iraqi Shi'ite cleric looks at the minaret of an ancient mosque near the Shi'ite holy city of Najaf. Joseph Eid/AFP/Getty Images

party in Iraq; a coalition of important Quraysh families in Mecca, including Muhammad's wife 'A'ishah and Talhah and Zubayr; and the party of Mu'awiyah, the governor of Syria and a member of 'Uthman's clan, the Banu Umayyah. Ostensibly the conflict focused on whether 'Uthman had been assassinated justly, whether 'Ali had been involved, and whether 'Uthman's death should be avenged by Mu'awiyah or by the leading Meccans. 'Ali and his party (*shi'ah*) at first gained power over the representatives of the other leading Meccan families, then lost it permanently to Mu'awiyah, who elevated Damascus, which had been his provincial capital, to the status of imperial capital. Disappointed at the Battle of Siffin (657) with 'Ali's failure to insist on his right to rule, a segment of his partisans withdrew; another segment of 'Ali's party intensified their loyalty to him as a just and heroic leader who was one of Muhammad's dearest intimates and the father of his only male descendants.

THE SECOND *FITNAH*

The second *fitnah* followed Mu'awiyah's caliphate (661–680), which itself was not free from strife, and coincided with the caliphates of Mu'awiyah's son Yazid I (ruled 680–683), whom he designated as successor, and Yazid's three successors. This *fitnah* was a second-generation reprise of the first; some of the personnel of the former were descendants or relatives of the leaders of the latter. Once again, different regions supported different claimants, as new tribal divisions emerged in the garrison towns; and once again, representatives of the Syrian Umayyads prevailed. In 680, at Karbala' in Iraq, Yazid's army murdered al-Husayn, a son of 'Ali and grandson of Muhammad, along with a small group of supporters, accusing them of rebellion. And even though the Umayyads subdued Iraq,

BATTLE OF SIFFIN

The series of negotiations and skirmishes during the first *fitnah* is known as the Battle of Siffin (May–July 657 CE). The battle and the arbitration that followed it undermined the authority of 'Ali as fourth caliph and prepared for the establishment of the Umayyad dynasty.

Mu'awiyah, governor of Syria, refused to recognize 'Ali as the new caliph before justice for the murder of his kinsman, the third caliph, 'Uthman, was done. For his part, 'Ali relied on the support of individuals who had been implicated in 'Uthman's murder and was therefore reluctant to prosecute them. 'Ali gathered support in Kufah, where he had established his centre, and invaded Syria. The two armies met along the Euphrates River at Siffin (near the Syrian-Iraqi border), where they engaged in an indecisive succession of skirmishes, truces, and battles, culminating in the legendary appearance of Mu'awiyah's troops with copies of the Qur'an impaled on their lances — supposedly a sign to let God's word decide the conflict. 'Ali agreed to bring the matter to arbitration on the basis of the Qur'an and delegated Abu Musa al-Ash'ari as his representative, while Mu'awiyah sent 'Amr ibn al-'As. By agreeing to arbitration, 'Ali conceded to deal with Mu'awiyah on equal terms, thus permitting him to challenge 'Ali's claim as leader of the Muslim community. This concession aroused the anger of a large group of 'Ali's followers, who protested that "judgment belongs to God alone" (Qur'an 6:57) and believed that arbitration would be a repudiation of the Qur'anic dictum "If one party rebels against the other, fight against that which rebels" (49:9). A small number of these pietists withdrew (*kharaju*) to the village of Harura' and so became known as Kharijites (Arabic: Khawarij).

Accounts of what precisely transpired at the arbitration vary; what is clear, however, is that 'Ali's position was critically weakened as a result. In May 658 Mu'awiyah was proclaimed caliph by some of his Syrian supporters. 'Ali and Mu'awiyah retained their own partisans, but, as Mu'awiyah's authority began to expand into Iraq and the Hejaz (western Saudi Arabia), 'Ali's diminished to Kufah, his capital. With 'Ali's assassination in 661, Mu'awiyah was free to establish himself as the first caliph of the Umayyad house.

rebellions in the name of this or that relative of 'Ali continued, attracting more and more non-Arab support and introducing new dimensions to his cause. In the Hejaz the Marwanid branch of the Umayyads, descendants of Marwan I who claimed the caliphate in 684, fought against 'Abd Allah ibn al-Zubayr for years; by the time they defeated him, they had lost most of Arabia to Kharijite rebels.

During the period of the first two *fitnah*s, resistance to Muslim rule was an added source of conflict. Some of this resistance took the form of syncretic or anti-Islamic religious movements. For example, during the second *fitnah*, in Iraq a Jew named Abu 'Isa al-'Isfahani led a syncretic movement (that is, a movement combining different forms of belief or practice) on the basis of his claim to be a prophet (an option not generally open to Muslim rebels) and forerunner of the messiah. He viewed Muhammad and Jesus as messengers sent not to all humanity but only to their own communities, so he urged each community to continue in its own tradition as he helped prepare for the coming of the messiah. In other areas, such as the newly conquered Maghrib, resistance took the form of large-scale military hostility. In the 660s the Umayyads had expanded their conflict with the Byzantine Empire by competing for bases in coastal North Africa; it soon became clear, however, that only a full-fledged occupation would serve their purposes. That occupation was begun by 'Uqbah ibn Nafi', the founder of al-Qayrawan (Kairouan, in modern Tunisia) and, as Sidi (Saint) 'Uqbah, the first of many Maghribi Muslim saints. It eventually resulted in the incorporation of large numbers of pagan or Christianized Amazigh (plural: Imazighen; Berber) tribes, the first large-scale forcible incorporation of tribal peoples since the secession of tribes under Abu Bakr. But first the Arab armies met fierce resistance from two individuals — one a man, Kusaylah, and one a woman, al-Kahinah — who became Amazigh heroes. Amazigh resistance was not controlled until the end of the 7th century, after which the Imazighen participated in the further conquest of the Maghrib and the Iberian Peninsula.

Thousands of Palestinian women pray in front of the Dome of the Rock during Ramadan in Jerusalem. Awad Awad/AFP/Getty Images

THE EMERGENT ISLAMIC CIVILIZATION

During the caliphate of 'Abd al-Malik ibn Marwan (ruled 685–705), which followed the end of the second *fitnah*, and under his successors during the next four decades, the problematic consequences of the conquests became much more visible. Like their Byzantine and late Sasanian predecessors, the Marwanid caliphs nominally ruled the various religious communities but allowed the communities' own appointed or elected officials to administer most internal affairs. Yet now the right of religious communities to live in this fashion was justified by the Qur'an and Sunnah; as peoples with revealed books (*ahl al-kitab*), they deserved protection (*dhimmah*) in return for a payment. The Arabs also formed a single religious community whose right to rule over the non-Arab protected communities the Marwanids sought to maintain.

To signify this supremacy, as well as his co-optation of previous legitimacy, 'Abd al-Malik ordered the construction of the monumental Dome of the Rock in Jerusalem, a major centre of non-Muslim population. The site chosen was sacred to Jews and Christians because of its associations with biblical history; it later gained added meaning for Muslims, who believed it to be the starting point for Muhammad's *mi'raj* (midnight journey to heaven). Although the Dome of the Rock (whose original function remains unclear) and many early mosques resembled contemporary Christian churches, gradually an Islamic aesthetic emerged: a dome on a geometrical base, accompanied by a minaret from which to deliver the call to prayer; and an emphasis on surface decoration that combined arabesque and geometrical design with calligraphic representations of God's Word. 'Abd al-Malik took other steps to mark the distinctiveness of Islamic rule: for example, he encouraged the use of Arabic as the language of

DOME OF THE ROCK

The Dome of the Rock (Arabic: Qubbat al-Sakhrah) is the oldest extant Islamic monument. The rock over which the shrine was built is sacred to both Muslims and Jews: the Prophet Muhammad is traditionally believed to have ascended into heaven from the site; and in Jewish tradition, it is here that Abraham, the progenitor and first patriarch of the Hebrew people, is said to have prepared to sacrifice his son Isaac. The Dome and Al-Aqsa Mosque are both located on the Temple Mount, the site of Solomon's Temple and its successors.

The original purpose of the Dome of the Rock, which was built between 685 and 691 CE by the caliph 'Abd al-Malik ibn Marwan, remains a source of debate. An unprecedented structure, it is virtually the first monumental building in Islamic history and is of considerable aesthetic and architectural importance; it is rich with mosaic, faience, and marble, much of which was added several centuries after its completion. Basically octagonal, the Dome of the Rock makes use of Byzantine techniques but is already distinctly Islamic. A wooden dome—approximately 60 feet (18 metres) in diameter and mounted on an elevated drum—rises above a circle of 16 piers and columns. Surrounding this circle is an octagonal arcade of 24 piers and columns. The outer walls repeat this octagon, each of the eight sides being approximately 60 feet (18 metres) wide and 36 feet (11 metres) high. Both the dome and the exterior walls contain many windows.

Christians and Muslims in the Middle Ages believed the Dome itself to be the Temple of Solomon (Templum Domini). The Knights Templar were quartered there in the Crusades, and Templar churches in Europe imitated its plan.

government and had Islamized coins minted to replace the Byzantine and Sasanian-style coinage that had continued to be used since the conquests. During the Marwanid period the Muslim community was further consolidated by the regularization of the public cult and the crystallization of a set of five minimal duties (sometimes called pillars).

The Marwanids also depended heavily on the help of non-Arab administrative personnel (*kuttab*, singular *katib*) and on administrative practices (e.g., a set of government bureaus) inherited from Byzantine and, in particular, late Sasanian practice. Pre-Islamic writings on governance translated into Arabic, especially from Middle Persian, influenced caliphal style. The governing structure at Damascus and in the provinces began to resemble pre-Islamic monarchy, and thus appealed to a majority of subjects, whose heritage extolled the absolute authority of a divinely sanctioned ruler. Much of the inspiration for this development came from 'Abd al-Malik's administrator in the eastern territories, al-Hajjaj ibn Yusuf al-Thaqafi, who was himself an admirer of Sasanian practice.

The Marwanid caliphs, as rulers of Muslims and non-Muslims alike, had thus been forced to respond to a variety of expectations. Ironically, it was their defense of the importance and distinctiveness of the Arabic language and the Islamic community, not their responsiveness to non-Muslim preferences, that prepared the way for the gradual incorporation of most of the subject population into the *ummah*. As the conquests slowed and the isolation of the fighters (*muqatilah*) became less necessary, it became more and more difficult to keep Arabs garrisoned. The sedentarization of Arabs that had begun in the Hejaz was being repeated and extended outside the peninsula. As the tribal links that had so dominated Umayyad politics began to break down, the meaningfulness of tying non-Arab converts to Arab tribes as clients was diluted; moreover, the number of non-Muslims who wished to join the *ummah* was already becoming too large for this process to work effectively.

Simultaneously, the growing prestige and elaboration of things Arabic and Islamic made them more attractive to non-Arab Muslims and to non-Muslims alike. The more the Muslim rulers succeeded, the more prestige their customs, norms, and habits acquired. Heirs to the considerable agricultural and commercial resources of the Nile-to-Oxus region, they increased its prosperity and widened its horizons by extending its control far to the east and west. Arabic, which occasionally had been used for administrative purposes in earlier empires, now became a valuable lingua franca. As Muslims continued to adapt to rapidly changing circumstances, they needed Arabic to reflect upon and elaborate what they had inherited from the Hejaz. Because the Qur'an, translation of which was prohibited, was written in a form of Arabic that quickly became archaic to Muslims living in the garrisons and because it contained references to life in Arabia before and during Muhammad's time, full understanding of the text required special effort. Scholars began to study the religion and poetry of the *jahiliyyah*, the times of ignorance before God's revelation to Muhammad. Philologians soon emerged, in the Hejaz as well as in the garrisons. Many Muslims cultivated reports, which came to be known as Hadith, of what Muhammad had said and done, in order to develop a clearer and fuller picture of his Sunnah. These materials were sometimes gathered into accounts of his campaigns, called *maghazi*. The emulation of Muhammad's Sunnah was a major factor in the development of recognizably "Muslim" styles of personal piety and public decision making. As differences in the garrisons needed to be settled according to "Islamic" principles, the caliphs appointed arbitrating judges, *qadi*s, who were knowledgeable in Qur'an and Sunnah. The pursuit of legal knowledge, *fiqh*, was taken up in many locales and informed by local pre-Islamic custom and Islamic resources. These special forms of knowledge began to be known as *'ulum* (singular *'ilm*) and the persons who pursued them as *ulama* (*'ulama'*, singular *'alim*), a role that provided new sources of prestige and influence, especially for recent converts or sons of converts.

Muslims outside Arabia were also affected by interacting with members of the religious communities over which they ruled. When protected non-Muslims converted, they brought new expectations and habits with them; Islamic eschatology is one area that reflects such enrichment. Unconverted protected groups (*dhimmis*) were equally influential. Expressions of Islamic identity often had to take into account the critique of non-Muslims, just as the various non-Muslim traditions were affected by contact with Muslims. This interaction had special consequences in the areas of prophethood and revelation, where major shifts and accommodations occurred among Jews, Christians, Mazdeans, and Muslims during the first two centuries of their coexistence. Muslims attempted to establish Muhammad's legitimacy as an heir to Jewish and Christian prophethood, while non-Muslims tried to distinguish their prophets and scriptures from Muhammad and the Qur'an. Within the emergent Islamicate civilization, the separate religious communities continued to go their own way, but the influence of Muslim rule and the intervention of the caliphs in their internal affairs could not help but affect them. The Babylonian Talmud, completed during these years, bears traces of early interaction among communities. In Iraq caliphal policy helped promote the Jewish gaons (local rabbinic authorities) over the exilarch (a central secular leader). Mazdeans turned to the Nestorian Church to avoid Islam, or reconceptualized Zoroaster as a prophet sent to a community with a Book. With the *dhimmi* system (the system of protecting non-Muslims for payment), Muslim rulers formalized and probably intensified pre-Islamic tendencies toward religious communalization. Furthermore, the greater formality of the new system could protect the subject communities from each other as well as from the dominant minority. So "converting" to Islam, at least in the Nile-to-Oxus region, meant joining one recognizably distinct social entity and leaving another. One of the most significant aspects of many Muslim societies was the inseparability of "religious" affiliation and group membership, a phenomenon that has translated poorly into the social structures of modern Muslim nations. In the central caliphal lands of the early 8th century, membership in the Muslim community offered the best chance for social and physical mobility, regardless of a certain degree of discrimination against non-Arabs. Among many astounding examples of this mobility is the fact that several of the early governors and independent dynasts of Egypt and the Maghrib were grandsons of men born in Central Asia.

The Marwanid Maghrib illustrates a kind of conversion more like that of the peninsular Arabs. After the defeat of initial Amazigh resistance movements, the Arab conquerors of the Maghrib quickly incorporated the Amazigh tribes en masse into the Muslim community, turning them immediately to further conquests. In 710 an Arab-Amazigh army set out for the Iberian Peninsula under the leadership of Tariq ibn Ziyad (the name Gibraltar is derived from Jabal Tariq, or "Mountain of Tariq"). They defeated King Roderick in 711; raided into and through the Iberian Peninsula, which they called al-Andalus; and ruled in the name of the Umayyad caliph. The Andalusian Muslims never had serious goals across the Pyrenees. In 732 Charles Martel encountered not a Muslim army but a summer raiding party; despite his "victory" over that party, Muslims continued their seasonal raiding along the southern French coast for many years. Muslim Andalusia is particularly interesting because there the pressure for large-scale conversion that was coming to plague the Umayyads in Syria, Iraq, and Iran never developed. Muslims may never have become a majority throughout their 700-year Andalusian presence. Non-Muslims entered into the Muslim realm as Mozarabs, Christians who had adopted the language and manners, rather than the faith, of the Arabs. Given essentially the same administrative arrangements, the Iberian Christian population was later restored to dominance while the Syrian Christian population was drastically reduced, but the Iberian Jewish population all but disappeared while the Nile-to-Oxus Jewish population survived.

The Imazighen who remained in the Maghrib illustrate the mobility of ideologies and institutions from the central lands to more recently conquered territories. No sooner had they given up anti-Muslim resistance and joined the Muslim community than they rebelled again, but this time an Islamic identity, Kharijism, provided the justification. Kharijite ideas had been carried to the Maghrib by refugees from the numerous revolts against the Marwanids. Kharijite egalitarianism suited the economic and social grievances of the Imazighen as non-Arab Muslims under Arab rule. The revolts outlasted the Marwanids; they resulted in the first independent Maghribi dynasty, the Rustamid, founded by Muslims of Persian descent. The direct influence of the revolts was felt as late as the 10th century and survives among small communities in Tunisia and Algeria.

THE THIRD *FITNAH*

Meanwhile, in the central caliphal lands, growing discontent with the emerging order crystallized in a multifaceted movement of opposition to the Marwanids. It culminated in the third *fitnah* (744–750), which resulted in the establishment of a new and final dynasty of caliphs, the 'Abbasids. Ever since the second *fitnah*, a number of concerned and self-conscious Muslims had begun to raise serious questions about the proper Muslim life and the Marwanids' ability to exemplify it, and to answer them by reference to key events in the *ummah*'s history. Pious Muslims tried to define a good Muslim and to decide whether a bad Muslim should be excluded from the community, or a bad caliph from office. They also considered God's role in determining a person's sinfulness and final dispensation. The proper relationship between Arab and non-Arab Muslims, and between Muslims and *dhimmis*, was another important and predictable focus of reflection. The willingness of non-Arabs to join the *ummah* was growing, but the Marwanids had not found a solution that was either ideologically acceptable or fiscally sound. Because protected non-Muslim groups paid special taxes, fiscal stability seemed to depend on continuing to discourage conversion. One Marwanid, 'Umar II (ruled 717–720), experimented unsuccessfully with a just solution. In these very practical and often pressing debates lay the germs of Muslim theology, as various overlapping positions, not always coterminous with political groupings, were taken: rejecting the history of the community by demanding rule by Muhammad's family; rejecting the history of the community by following any pious Muslim and excluding any sinner; or accepting the history of the community, its leaders, and most of its members.

In the course of these debates the Marwanid caliphs began to seem severely deficient to a significant number of Muslims of differing persuasions and aspirations. Direct and implied criticism began to surface. Al-Hasan al-Basri, a pious ascetic and a model for the early Sufis, called on the Marwanids to rule as good Muslims and called on good

Muslims to be suspicious of worldly power. Ibn Ishaq composed an account of Muhammad's messengership that emphasized the importance of the *ansar*, the Yathribi tribes that accepted Muhammad, and by implication the non-Arab converts (from whom Ibn Ishaq himself was descended). The Marwanids were accused of *bid'ah*, new actions for which there were no legitimate Islamic precedents. Their continuation of pre-Islamic institutions — the spy system, extortion of deposed officials by torture, and summary execution—were some of their most visible "offenses." To the pious, the ideal ruler, or imam (the word also for a Muslim who led the *salat*), should, like Muhammad, possess special learning and knowledge. The first four caliphs, they argued, had been imams in this sense, but under the Umayyads the caliphate had been reduced to a military and administrative office devoid of *imamah*, of true legitimacy. This piety-minded opposition to the Umayyads, as it has been aptly dubbed, now began to talk about a new dispensation. Some of the most vocal members found special learning and knowledge only in Muhammad's family. Some defined Muhammad's family broadly to include any Hashimite; others, more narrowly, to include only descendants of 'Ali. As the number of Muhammad's descendants through 'Ali had grown, numerous rebellions had broken out in the name of one or the other, drawing on various combinations of constituencies and reflecting a wide spectrum of Islamic and pre-Islamic aspirations.

In the late Marwanid period, the piety-minded opposition found expression in a movement organized in Khorasan (Khurasan) by Abu Muslim, a semisecret operative of one particularly ambitious Hashimite family, the 'Abbasids. The 'Abbasids, who were kin but not descendants of Muhammad, claimed also to have inherited, a generation earlier, the authority of one of 'Ali's actual descendants,

Abu Hashim. Publicly Abu Muslim called for any qualified member of Muhammad's family to become caliph, but privately he allowed the partisans (*shi'ah*) of 'Ali to assume that he meant them. Abu Muslim ultimately succeeded because he managed to link the concerns of the piety-minded in Syria and Iraq with Khorasanian discontent. He played upon the grievances of its Arab tribes against the tribes of Syria and their representatives in the Khorasanian provincial government, and on the millennial expectations of non-Arab converts and non-Muslims disenchanted with the injustices of Marwanid rule.

When in 750 the army organized and led by Abu Muslim succeeded in defeating the last Marwanid ruler, his caliph-designate represented only one segment of this broad coalition. He was the head of the 'Abbasid family, Abu al-'Abbas al-Saffah, who now subordinated the claims of the party of 'Ali to those of his own family and who promised to restore the unity of the *ummah*, or *jama'ah*. The circumstances of his accession reconfigured the piety-minded opposition that had helped bring him to power. The party of 'Ali refused to accept the compromise the 'Abbasids offered. Their former fellow opponents did accept membership in the reunified *jama'ah*, isolating the People of the Shi'ah and causing them to define themselves in terms of more radical points of view. Those who accepted the early 'Abbasids came to be known as the People of the Sunnah and Jama'ah. They accepted the cumulative historical reality of the *ummah*'s first century: all the decisions of the community and all the caliphs it had accepted had been legitimate, as would be any subsequent caliph who could unite the community. The concept of *fitnah* acquired a fully historicist meaning: if internal discord were a trial sent by God, then any unifying victor must be God's choice.

SUNNIS AND SHI'ITES

The historicists came to be known as Sunnis and their main opponents as Shi'ites. These labels are somewhat misleading because they imply that only the Sunnis tried to follow the Sunnah of Muhammad. In fact, each group relied on the Sunnah, but emphasized different elements. For the Sunnis, who should more properly be called the Jama'i-Sunnis, the principle of solidarity was essential to the Sunnah. The Shi'ites argued that the fundamental element of the Sunnah, and one willfully overlooked by the Jama'i-Sunnis, was Muhammad's devotion to his family and his wish that they succeed him through 'Ali. These new labels expressed and consolidated the social reorganization that had been under way since the beginning of the conquests. The vast majority of Muslims now became consensus-oriented, while a small minority became oppositional. The inherent inimitability of Muhammad's role had made it impossible for any form of successorship to capture universal approval.

When the 'Abbasids denied the special claims of the family of 'Ali, they prompted the Shi'ites to define themselves as a permanent opposition to the status quo. The crystallization of Shi'ism into a movement of protest received its greatest impetus during and just after the lifetime of one of the most influential Shi'ite leaders of the early 'Abbasid period, Ja'far al-Sadiq (died 765). Ja'far's vision and leadership allowed the Shi'ites to understand their chaotic history as a meaningful series of efforts by truly pious and suffering Muslims to right the wrongs of the majority. The leaders of the minority had occupied the office of imam, the central Shi'ite institution, which had been passed on from the first imam, 'Ali, by designation down to Ja'far, the sixth. To protect his followers from increasing Sunni hostility to the views of radical Shi'ites, known as the *ghulat* ("extremists"), who claimed prophethood for 'Ali, Ja'far made a distinction that both protected the uniqueness of prophethood and established the superiority of the role of imam. Since prophethood had ended, its true intent would die without the imams, whose protection from error allowed them to carry out their indispensable task.

Although Ja'far did develop an ideology that invited Sunni toleration, he did not unify all Shi'ites. Differences continued to be expressed through loyalty to various of his relatives. During Ja'far's lifetime, his uncle Zayd revolted in Kufah (740), founding the branch of Shi'ism known as the Zaydiyyah (Zaydis), or Fivers (for their allegiance to the fifth imam), who became particularly important in southern Arabia. Any pious follower of 'Ali could become their imam, and any imam could be deposed if he behaved unacceptably. The Shi'ite majority followed Ja'far's son Musa al-Kazim and imams in his line through the 12th, who disappeared in 873. Those loyal to the 12 imams became known as the Imamis or Ithna 'Ashariyyah (Twelvers). They adopted a quietistic stance toward the status quo government of the 'Abbasids and prepared to wait until the 12th imam should return as the messiah to avenge injustices against Shi'ites and to restore justice before the Last Judgment. Some of Ja'far's followers, however, remained loyal to Isma'il, Ja'far's eldest son who predeceased his father after being designated. These became the Isma'iliyyah (Isma'ilis) or Sab'iyyah (Seveners), and they soon became a source of continuing revolution in the name of Isma'il's son Muhammad al-Tamm, who was believed to have disappeared. Challenges to the 'Abbasids were not long in coming. Of particular significance was the establishment in 789 of the first independent Shi'ite dynasty, in present-day Morocco,

Fifteenth-century vellum by a Persian artist depicting Harun al-Rashid and a barber in a Turkish bath. Or.6810 f.27v/British Library, London, UK/© British Library Board. All Rights Reserved/The Bridgeman Art Library

by Idris ibn 'Abd Allah ibn Hasan II, who had fled after participating in an unsuccessful uprising near Mecca. Furthermore, Kharijite rebellions continued to occur regularly.

THE 'ABBASIDS

Legitimacy was a scarce and fragile resource in all pre-modern societies; in the early 'Abbasid environment, competition to define and secure legitimacy was especially intense. The 'Abbasids came to power vulnerable; their early actions undermined the unitive potential of their office. Having alienated the Shi'ites, they liquidated the Umayyad family, one of whom, 'Abd al-Rahman I, escaped and founded his own state in Andalusia. Although the 'Abbasids were able to buttress their legitimacy by employing the force of their Khorasanian army, by appealing to their piety-minded support, and by emphasizing their position as heirs to the pre-Islamic traditions of rulership, their own circumstances and policies militated against them. Despite their continuing preference for Khorasanian troops, the 'Abbasids' move to Iraq and their execution of Abu Muslim disappointed the Khorasanian chauvinists who had helped them. The non-Muslim majority often rebelled too. Bih'afrid ibn Farwardin claimed to be a prophet capable of incorporating both Mazdeism and Islam into a new faith. Hashim ibn Hakim, called al-Muqanna' ("the Veiled One"), around 759 declared himself a prophet and then a god, heir to all previous prophets, to numerous followers of 'Ali, and to Abu Muslim himself.

The 'Abbasids symbolized their connection with their pre-Islamic predecessors by founding a new capital, Baghdad, near the old Sasanian capital. They also continued to elaborate the Sasanian-like structure begun by the Marwanid governors in Iraq. Their court life became more and more elaborate, the bureaucracy fuller, the inner sanctum of the palace fuller than ever with slaves and concubines as well as the retinues of the caliph's four legal wives. By the time of Harun al-Rashid (ruled 786–809), Europe had nothing to compare with Baghdad, not even the court of his contemporary Charlemagne (ruled 768–814). But problems surfaced too. Slaves' sons fathered by Muslims were not slaves and so could compete for the succession. Despite the 'Abbasids' defense of Islam, unconverted Jews and Christians could be influential at court. The head (vizier, or *wazir*) of the financial bureaucracy sometimes became the effective head of government by taking over the chancery as well. Like all absolute rulers, the 'Abbasid caliphs soon confronted the insoluble dilemma of absolutism: the monarch cannot be absolute unless he depends on helpers, but his dependence on helpers undermines his absolutism. Harun al-Rashid experienced this paradox in a particularly painful way: having drawn into his service prominent members of a family of Buddhist converts, the Barmakids, he found them such rivals that he liquidated them within a matter of years. It was also during Harun's reign that Ibrahim ibn al-Aghlab, a trusted governor in Tunis, founded a dynasty that gradually became independent, as did the Tahirids, the 'Abbasid governors in Khorasan, two decades later.

The 'Abbasids' ability to rival their pre-Islamic predecessors was enhanced by their generous patronage of artists and artisans of all kinds. The great 7,000-mile (11,265–km) Silk Road from Ch'ang-an (now Xi'an [Sian], China) to Baghdad—then the two largest cities in the world—helped provide the wealth. The ensuing literary florescence was promoted by the capture of a group of Chinese papermakers at the Battle of Talas in 751. The 'Abbasids encouraged translation from pre-Islamic languages, particularly Middle Persian, Greek, and Syriac. This activity provided a channel through which older thought could enter and be reoriented by Islamicate societies. In the field of mathematics, al-Khwarizmi, from whose name the word *algorithm* is derived, creatively combined Hellenistic and Sanskritic concepts. The word

HARUN AL-RASHID

Harun al-Rashid (ruled 786–809; in full, Harun al-Rashid ibn Muhammad al-Mahdi ibn al-Mansur al-'Abbasi) was the son of al-Mahdi, the third 'Abbasid caliph (ruled 775–785). His mother, al-Khayzuran, was a former slave girl from Yemen and a woman of strong personality who greatly influenced affairs of state in the reigns of her husband and sons. In 780 and 782 Harun was nominal leader of expeditions against the Byzantine Empire, though the military decisions were doubtless made by the experienced generals accompanying him. The expedition of 782 reached the Bosporus, opposite Constantinople, and peace was concluded on favourable terms. For this success Harun received the honorific title of al-Rashid, "the one following the right path," and was named second in succession to the throne and appointed governor of Tunisia, Egypt, Syria, Armenia, and Azerbaijan, with his tutor, Yahya the Barmakid, acting as actual administrator. After a brief period of rule by his elder brother al-Hadi, Harun al-Rashid became caliph in September 786, with Yahya as his vizier.

The fabulous descriptions of Harun and his court in *The Thousand and One Nights* are idealized and romanticized, yet they had a considerable basis in fact. Untold wealth had flowed into the new capital of Baghdad since its foundation in 762. The leading men, and still more their wives, vied in conspicuous consumption, and in Harun's reign this reached levels unknown before. Harun's palace was an enormous institution, with numerous eunuchs, concubines, singing girls, and male and female servants. He himself was a connoisseur of music and poetry and gave lavish gifts to outstanding musicians and poets. In the stories of his nocturnal wanderings through Baghdad in disguise, he is usually accompanied by Masrur the executioner as well as friends like Ja'far the Barmakid (Yahya's son) and Abu Nuwas, the brilliant poet.

The less pleasant aspects of Harun's character are highlighted by the fall of the Barmakids, who for more than 16 years had been mainly responsible for the administration of the empire and who had provided the money for the luxury and extravagance of the court. Moreover, Ja'far the Barmakid had become Harun's special friend, so that gossip spoke of a homosexual relationship. Gossip also alleged that Harun had arranged that Ja'far should secretly marry his sister 'Abbasah, on condition that he did not consummate the marriage, but Ja'far fell in love with her, and she had a child. Whether in anger at this or not, Harun had Ja'far executed on Jan. 29, 803. The other members of the family were imprisoned and their goods confiscated. Modern historians reject this gossip and instead suggest that Harun felt dominated by the Barmakids and may even have coveted their wealth. Moreover, diverse interests within the empire were being attracted to two opposing poles. On the one side were the "secretaries," or civil servants, many Persians, and many men from the eastern provinces; on the other side were the religious scholars (*ulama*), many Arabs, and many from the western provinces. Since the Barmakids favoured the first group of interests and the new vizier, al-Fadl ibn al-Rabi', favoured the second, it is likely that this political cleavage was involved in the change of ministry.

The struggle between the two groups of interests continued for at least half a century. Harun recognized its existence by assigning Iraq and the western provinces to his son al-Amin, the heir apparent, and the eastern provinces to the second in succession, his son al-Ma'mun. The former was son of the Arab princess Zubaydah and after 803 had al-Fadl ibn al-Rabi' as tutor. Al-Ma'mun was son of a Persian slave girl and after 803 had as tutor a Barmakid protégé, al-Fadl ibn Sahl. Harun has been criticized for so dividing the empire and contributing to its disintegration, for there was war between his two sons after his death; but it may well be that by making the cleavage manifest, he contributed to its eventual resolution after 850.

algebra derives from the title of his major work, *Kitab al-jabr wa al-muqabalah* ("The Book of Integration and Equation"). Movements such as *falsafah* (a combination of the positive sciences with logic and metaphysics) and *kalam* (systematic theological discourse) applied Hellenistic thought to new questions. The translation of Indo-Persian lore promoted the development of *adab*, a name for a sophisticated prose literature as well as the set of refined urbane manners that characterized its clientele. Soon a movement called *shu'ubiyyah* arose to champion the superiority of non-Arabic tastes over the alleged crudeness of the poetry so dear to Arabic litterateurs. However, the great writer of early 'Abbasid times, al-Jahiz, produced a type of *adab* that fused pre-Islamic and Islamic concerns in excellent Arabic style. Many of these extra-Islamic resources conflicted with Islamic expectations. Ibn al-Muqaffa', an administrator under al-Mansur (ruled 754–775), urged his master to emulate pre-Islamic models, lest the law that the religious specialists (the *ulama*) were developing undermine caliphal authority irrevocably.

The 'Abbasids never acted on such advice completely; they even contravened it by appealing for piety-minded support. Having encouraged conversion, they tried to "purify" the Muslim community of what they perceived to be socially dangerous and alien ideas. Al-Mahdi (ruled 775–785) actively persecuted the Manichaeans, whom he defined as heretics so as to deny them status as a protected community. He also tried to identify Manichaeans who had joined the Muslim community without abandoning their previous ideas and practices. 'Abbasid "purification of Islam" ironically coincided with some of the most significant absorption of pre-Islamic monotheistic lore to date, as illustrated by the stories of the prophets written by Al-Kisa'i, grammarian and tutor to a royal prince. Even though, like the Marwanids, the 'Abbasids continued to maintain administrative courts, not accessible to the *qadi*s, they also promoted the study of *'ilm* and the status of those who pursued it. In so doing they fostered what Ibn al-Muqaffa' had feared—the emergence of an independent body of law, Shari'ah, which Muslims could use to evaluate and circumvent caliphal rule itself.

Shari'ah

A key figure in the development of Shari'ah was Abu 'Abd Allah al-Shafi'i, who died in 820. By his time Islamic law was extensive but uncoordinated, reflecting differing local needs and tastes. Schools had begun to form around various recognized masters, such as al-Awza'i in Syria, Abu Hanifah in Iraq, and Malik ibn Anas, all of whom used some combination of local custom, personal reasoning, Qur'an, and Hadith. Al-Shafi'i was raised in Mecca, studied with Malik, participated in a Shi'ite revolt in the Yemen, and was sent to Baghdad as a prisoner of the caliph. After his release he emigrated to Egypt, where he produced his most famous work. Like most other *faqih*s (students of jurisprudence, or *fiqh*), al-Shafi'i viewed Muhammad's community as a social ideal and his first four successors as rightly guided. So that this exemplary time could provide the basis for Islamic law, he constructed a hierarchy of legal sources: Qur'an; Hadith, clearly traceable to Muhammad and in some cases to his companions; *ijma'* (consensus); and *qiyas* (analogy to one of the first three).

The way in which Islamic law had developed had allowed many pre-Islamic customs, such as the veiling and seclusion of women, to receive a sanction not given to them in the Qur'an or Hadith. Al-Shafi'i did not change that entirely. Law continued to be pursued in different centres, and several major "ways" (*madhhabs*) began to coalesce among Sunnis and Shi'ites alike. Among Sunnis, four schools came to be preeminent—Shafi'iyyah (Shafiites), Malikiyyah (Malikites), Hanafiyyah (Hanafites), and Hanabilah (Hanbalites)—and each individual Muslim was expected to restrict himself to only one. Furthermore, the notion that the gate of *ijtihad* (personal effort at reasoning) closed in the 9th century was not firmly established until the 12th century. However, al-Shafi'i's system was widely influential in controlling divergence and in limiting undisciplined forms of personal reasoning. It also stimulated the collecting and testing of hadiths for their unbroken traceability to Muhammad or a companion. The need to verify Hadith stimulated a characteristic form of premodern Muslim intellectual and literary activity, the collecting of biographical materials into compendiums (*tabaqat*). By viewing the Qur'an and documentable Sunnah as preeminent, al-Shafi'i also undermined those in 'Abbasid court circles who wanted a more flexible base from which the caliph could operate. The Shari'ah came to be a supremely authoritative, comprehensive set of norms and rules covering every aspect of life, from worship to personal hygiene. It applied equally to all Muslims, including the ruler, whom Shari'ah-minded Muslims came to view as its protector, not its administrator or developer. While the caliphs were toying with theocratic notions of themselves as the shadow of God on Earth, the students of legal knowledge were defining their rule as "nomocratic," based only on the law they protected and enforced.

According to the Shari'ah, a Muslim order was one in which the ruler was Muslim and the Shari'ah was enshrined as a potential guide to all; Muslims were one confessional community among many, each of which would have its own laws that would apply except in disputes between members of different communities. The Shari'ah regulated relations and inequities among different segments of society—freeborn Muslim, slave, and protected non-Muslim. The process that produced Shari'ah resembled the evolution of oral Torah and rabbinic law, which the

Shari'ah resembled in its comprehensiveness, egalitarianism, and consensualism, in its absorption of local custom, in its resistance to distinguishing the sublime from the mundane, and in its independence from government. Like many Jews, many ultra-pious Muslims came to view the law as a divine rather than human creation.

THE FOURTH *FITNAH*

During the reign of al-Ma'mun (813–833) the implications of all this *'ilm*-based activity for caliphal authority began to become clear. Al-Ma'mun came to the caliphate as the result of the fourth *fitnah*, which reflected the persisting alienation of Khorasan. Al-Ma'mun's father, Harun al-Rashid, provided for the empire to be divided at his death between two sons. Al-Amin would rule in the capital and all the western domains, and al-Ma'mun, from his provincial seat at Merv in Khorasan, would rule the less significant east. When Harun died, his sons struggled to expand their control. Al-Ma'mun won. During his reign, which probably represents the high point of caliphal absolutism, the court intervened in an unprecedented manner in the intellectual life of its Muslim subjects, who for the next generation engaged in the first major intra-Muslim conflict that focused on belief as well as practice. The Muslims, who now constituted a much more sizable proportion of the population but whose faith lacked doctrinal clarity, began to engage in an argument reminiscent of 2nd-century Christian discussions of the Logos. Among Christians, for whom the Word was Jesus, the argument had taken a Christological form. But for Muslims the argument had to centre on the Qur'an and its created or uncreated nature. Al-Ma'mun, as well as his brother and successor al-Mu'tasim (833–842), was attracted to the Mu'tazilah

(Mutazilites), whose school had been influenced by Hellenistic ideas as well as by contact with non-Muslim theologians. If the Qur'an were eternal along with God, his unity would, for the Mu'tazilah, be violated. They especially sought to avoid literal exegesis of the Qur'an, which in their view discouraged free will and produced embarrassing inconsistencies and anthropomorphisms. By arguing that the Qur'an was created in time, they could justify metaphorical and changing interpretation. By implication, Muhammad's position as deliverer of revelation was undermined because Hadith was made less authoritative.

The opponents of the Mu'tazilah, and therefore of the official position, coalesced around the figure of Ahmad ibn Hanbal. A leading master of Hadith, he had many followers, some of them recent converts, whom he was able to mobilize in large public demonstrations against the doctrine of the created Qur'an. Because viewing the Qur'an as created would invalidate its absolute authority, Ibn Hanbal argued for an eternal Qur'an and emphasized the importance of Muhammad's Sunnah to the understanding of it. By his time, major literary works had established a coherent image of the indispensability of Muhammad's prophethood. In fact, just before the Mu'tazilite controversy began, Ibn Hisham had produced his classic recension of the *sirah*, or life, of Muhammad, composed half a century earlier by Ibn Ishaq. As in the early Christian church, these were not merely dogmatic issues. They were rooted in the way ordinary Muslims lived, just as affection for a divine Christ had become popular sentiment by the time Arius and Athanasius debated. Although Muslims lacked an equivalent of the Christian church, they resolved these issues similarly; like Jesus for the Christians, the Qur'an for the Muslims was somehow part of God. Hadith-mindedness and emulation of Muhammad's Sunnah had become such an essential part of the daily life of ordinary people that the Mu'tazilite position, as intellectually consistent and attractive as it was, was unmarketable. In a series of forcible inquiries called *mihnah*, al-Ma'mun and al-Mu'tasim actively persecuted those who, like Ibn Hanbal, would not conform, but popular sentiment triumphed, and after al-Mu'tasim's death the caliph al-Mutawakkil was forced to reverse the stand of his predecessors.

This caliphal failure to achieve doctrinal unity coincided with other crises. By al-Mu'tasim's reign the tribal troops were becoming unreliable and the Tahirid governors of Khorasan more independent. Al-Mu'tasim expanded his use of military slaves, finding them more loyal but more unruly too. Soon he had to house them at Samarra', a new capital north of Baghdad, where the caliphate remained until 892. For most of this period, the caliphs were actually under the control of their slave soldiery, and, even though they periodically reasserted their authority, rebellions continued. Many were anti-Muslim, like that of the Iranian Babak (whose 20-year-long revolt was crushed in 837), but increasingly they were intra-Muslim, like the Kharijite-led revolt of black agricultural slaves (Zanj) in southern Iraq (869–883). By 870 then, the Baghdad-Samarra' caliphate had become one polity among many; its real rulers had no ideological legitimacy. At Córdoba the Umayyads had declared their independence, and the Maghrib was divided among several dynasties of differing persuasions — the Shi'ite Idrisids, the Kharijite Rustamids, and the Jama'i-Sunni Aghlabids. The former governors of the 'Abbasids, the Tulunids, ruled Egypt and parts of Arabia. Iran was divided between the Saffarids, governors of the 'Abbasids in the south, and the Persian Samanids in the north.

The centrifugal forces represented by these administrative divisions should not obscure, however, the existence of numerous centripetal forces that continued to give Islamdom, from Andalusia to Central Asia, other types of unity. The ideal of the caliphate continued to be a source of unity after the reality waned; among all the new states, no alternative to the caliphate could replace it. Furthermore, now that Muslims constituted a majority almost everywhere in Islamdom, conflict began to be expressed almost exclusively in Islamic rather than anti-Islamic forms. In spite of continuing intra-Muslim conflict, Muslim worship and belief remained remarkably uniform. The annual pilgrimage to Mecca helped reinforce this underlying unity by bringing disparate Muslims together in a common rite. The pilgrimage, as well as the rise of prosperous regional urban centres, enhanced the trade that traversed Islamdom regardless of political conflicts. Along the trade routes that crisscrossed Eurasia, Islamdom at its centre, moved not only techniques and goods but ideas as well. A network of credit and banking, caravansaries, and intercity mercantile alliances tied far-flung regions together. Central was the caravan, then the world's most effective form of transport. The peripatetic nature of education promoted cross-fertilization. Already the *faqir* (fakir), a wandering mendicant Sufi dervish, was a familiar traveler. Across Islamdom, similar mosque-market complexes sprang up in most towns; because municipal institutions were rare, political stability so unpredictable, and government intervention kept to a minimum (sometimes by design, more often by necessity), the Shari'ah and the learned men who carried it became a mainstay of everyday life and social intercourse. The Shari'ah, along with the widespread affection for the Sunnah of Muhammad, regulated, at least among pious Muslims, personal habits of the most specific sort, from the use of

AL-BUKHARI

One of the greatest Muslim compilers and scholars of Hadith (the recorded corpus of the sayings and acts of the Prophet Muhammad), al-Bukhari (810–870) began learning the utterances and actions of the Prophet by heart while still a child. His travels in search of more information about them began with a pilgrimage to Mecca when he was 16. He then went to Egypt, and for 16 years he sought out informants from Cairo to Merv in Central Asia. Al-Bukhari was an extremely scrupulous compiler, showing great critical discrimination and editorial skill in his selection of traditions as authentic ones. From the approximately 600,000 traditions he gathered, he selected only about 7,275 that he deemed completely reliable and thus meriting inclusion in his *Al-Jami' al-Sahih* ("The Authentic Collection"). He arranged his collection in sections according to subject so that the reader can compare the soundest accounts of the Prophet's example, in word or deed, on points of law and religious doctrine as diverse as the validity of good deeds performed before conversion to Islam and marriage law.

As a preliminary to his *Sahih*, al-Bukhari wrote *Al-Ta'rikh al-kabir* ("The Large History"), which contains biographies of the persons forming the living chain of oral transmission and recollection of traditions back to the Prophet. Toward the end of his life, he was involved in a theological dispute in Nishapur and left that city for Bukhara, but, following his refusal to give special classes for Bukhara's governor and his children, he was forced into exile in Khartank, a village near Samarkand.

scent to the cut of a beard. Comprehensive and practical, the Sunnah could amuse as well. When asked whether to trust in God or tie one's camel, so a popular hadith goes, the Prophet replied, "Trust in God, then tie your camel."

The significance of Hadith and Sunnah is represented by the ending date of the period of conversion and crystallization. No one can say exactly when the majority of Islamdom's population became Muslim. Older scholarship looks to the end of the first quarter of the 9th century, newer scholarship to the beginning of the third quarter. In 870 a man died whose life's work symbolized the consolidation of Islam in everyday life: al-Bukhari, who produced one of the six collections of Hadith recognized as authoritative by Jama'i-Sunni Muslims. His fellow collector of Hadith, Muslim ibn al-Hajjaj, died about four years later. About the same time, classical thinkers in other areas of Islamicate civilization died, among them the great author of *adab*, al-Jahiz (died 868/869), the great early ecstatic Sufis Abu al-Fayd Dhu al-Nun al-Misri (died 861) and Abu Yazid Bistami (died 874), the philosopher Ya'qub ibn Ishaq al-Sabah al-Kindi (died *c.* 870), and the historian of the conquests al-Baladhuri (died *c.* 892). Men of different religious and ethnic heritages, they signified by the last quarter of the 9th century the full and varied range of intellectual activities of a civilization that had come of age.

CHAPTER 4

FRAGMENTATION AND FLORESCENCE (870–1041)

T he unifying forces operative at the end of the period of conversion and crystallization persisted during the period of fragmentation and florescence, but the caliphal lands in Iraq became less central. Even though Baghdad remained preeminent in cultural prestige, important initiatives were being taken from surrounding "regions": Andalusia; the Maghrib and sub-Saharan Africa; Egypt, Syria, and the holy cities (Mecca and Medina); Iraq; and Iran, Afghanistan, Transoxania, and, toward the end of the period, northern India.

THE RISE OF COMPETITIVE REGIONS

The rise of competitive regions signified a number of important realities. Increasingly, regional courts could compete with the 'Abbasids and with each other as patrons of culture. Interregional and intraregional conflicts were often couched in terms of loyalties formed in the period of conversion and crystallization, but local history provided supplemental identities. Although the 'Abbasid caliphate was still a focus of concern and debate, other forms of leadership became important. Just as being Muslim no longer meant being Arab, being cultured no longer meant speaking and writing exclusively in Arabic. Certain Muslims began to cultivate a second language of high culture, New Persian. As in pre-Islamic times, written as well as spoken bilingualism became important. Ethnic differences were blurred by the effects of peripatetic education and shared languages. Physical mobility was so common that many individuals lived and died far from their places of birth. Cultural creativity was so noticeable that this period is often called the Renaissance of Islam.

Economic changes also promoted regional strengths. Although Baghdad continued to profit from its central location, caliphal neglect of Iraq's irrigation system and southerly shifts in the trans-Asian trade promoted the fortunes of Egypt. The opening of the Sahara to Maghribi Muslims provided a new source of slaves, salt, and minerals; and Egyptian expansion into the Mediterranean opened a major channel for Islamicate influence on medieval Europe. Islamdom continued to expand, sometimes as the result of aggression on the part of frontier warriors (*ghazis*) but more often as the result of trade. The best symbol of this expansiveness is Ibn Fadlan, who left a provocative account of his mission in 921, on behalf of the Baghdad caliph, to the Volga Bulgars, among whom he met Swedes coming down the river to trade.

By the beginning of the period of fragmentation and florescence, the subject populations of most Muslim rulers were predominantly Muslim, and nonsedentary peoples had ceased to play a major role. The period gave way to a much longer period (dated 1041–1405) in which migratory tribal peoples were once again critically important. In 1041 the reign of the Ghaznavid sultan Mas'ud I ended. By then the Ghaznavid state had lost control over the Seljuq Turks in their eastern Iranian domains and thus inaugurated Islamdom's second era of tribal expansion. Because localism and cosmopolitanism coexisted in the period of fragmentation and florescence, the period is best approached through a region-by-region survey that underscores phenomena of interregional significance.

ANDALUSIA, THE MAGHRIB, AND SUB-SAHARAN AFRICA

Andalusia, far from the centre of Islamdom, illustrated the extent of 'Abbasid prestige and the assertion of local creativity. In the beginning of the period, Islamicate rule was represented by the Umayyads at Córdoba. Established in 756 by 'Abd al-Rahman I (known as al-Dakhil, "the Immigrant"), a refugee from the 'Abbasid victory over the Syrian Umayyads, the Umayyad dynasty in Córdoba replaced a string of virtually independent deputies of the Umayyad governors in the Maghrib. At first the Cordoban Umayyads had styled themselves emirs, the title also used by caliphal governors and other local rulers. Though refugees from 'Abbasid hostility, they continued to mention the 'Abbasids in the salat al-jum'ah (Friday prayer) until 773. Their independence was not made official, however, until their best-known member, 'Abd al-Rahman III (ruled 912–961), adopted the title of caliph in 929 and began having the Friday prayer recited in the name of his own house.

The fact that 'Abd al-Rahman declared his independence from the 'Abbasids while he modeled his court after theirs illustrates the period's cultural complexities. Like that of the 'Abbasids and the Marwanids, 'Abd al-Rahman's absolute authority was limited by the nature of his army

'ABD AL-RAHMAN I

'Abd al-Rahman I (flourished 750–788) was a member of the Umayyad ruling family of Syria who founded an Umayyad dynasty in Spain. When the 'Abbasids overthrew the Umayyad caliphate in 750 CE and sought to kill as many members of the Umayyad family as possible, 'Abd al-Rahman fled, eventually reaching Spain. The Iberian Peninsula had for some time been occupied by Muslim Arab forces, and he recognized political opportunity for himself in the rivalries of the Qays and Yaman, the dominant Arab factions there. By shifting alliances and using mercenary support, he placed himself in a position of power, attacking and defeating the governor of Al-Andalus in 756 and making Córdoba his capital. As news of his success spread eastward, men who had previously worked in the Umayyad administrative system came to Spain to work with 'Abd al-Rahman, and his administrative system came to resemble that formerly operative in Damascus. 'Abd al-Rahman secured his realm against external attack by defeating armies sent by Charlemagne and the 'Abbasid caliph. Although he faced a series of rebellions by Muslim Spaniards, Imazighen (Berbers) from the mountainous areas, and various Arab clans, his authority and dynasty remained firmly in power.

(Amazigh tribesmen and Slav slaves) and by his dependence on numerous assistants. His internal problems were compounded by external threats, from the Christian kingdoms in the north and the Fatimids in the Maghrib. The Umayyad state continued to be the major Muslim presence in the peninsula until 1010, after which time it became, until 1031, but one of many independent city-states. Nowhere is the connection between fragmentation and florescence more evident than in the courts of these *muluk al-tawa'if*, or "party kings"; it was they who patronized some of Andalusia's most brilliant Islamicate culture. This

Moorish arches from Medina Azahàra (Madinat al-Zahra) Palace, built during the reign of 'Abd al-Rahman III. Remains of this large, luxurious testament to the caliph's power sit outside of Cordoba, Spain. Xavi Gomez/ Hulton Archive/Getty Images

florescence also demonstrated the permeability of the Muslim-Christian frontier. For example, the poet and theologian Ibn Hazm (994–1064) composed love poetry, such as *Tawq al-hamamah* (*The Ring of the Dove*), which may have contributed to ideas of chivalric love among the Provençal troubadours.

In 870 the Maghrib was divided among several dynasties, all but one of foreign origin and only one of which, the Aghlabids, nominally represented the 'Abbasids. The Muslim Arabs had been very different rulers than any of their predecessors—Phoenicians, Romans, Vandals, or Byzantines—who had occupied but not settled. Their interests in North Africa had been secondary to their objectives in the Mediterranean, so they had restricted themselves to coastal settlements, which they used as staging points for trade with the western Mediterranean or as sources of food for their "metropolitan" population.

They had separated themselves from the Imazighen with a fortified frontier. The Arabs, however, forced away from the coast in order to compete more effectively with the Byzantines, had quickly tried to incorporate the Imazighen, who were also pastoralists. One branch of the Imazighen, the Sanhajah, extended far into the Sahara, across which they had established a caravan trade with blacks in the Sudanic belt. At some time in the 10th century the Sanhajah nominally converted to Islam, and their towns in the Sahara began to assume Muslim characteristics. Around 990 a black kingdom in the Sudan, Ghana, extended itself as far as Audaghost, the Sanhajah centre in the Sahara. Thus was black Africa first brought into contact with the Muslim Mediterranean, and thus were the conditions set for dramatic developments in the Maghrib during the 12th and 13th centuries.

In the late 9th century the Maghrib was unified and freed from outside control for the first time. Paradoxically, this independence was achieved by outsiders associated with an international movement of political activism and subversion. Driven underground by 'Abbasid intolerance and a maturing ideology of covert revolutionism, the Isma'ili Shi'ites had developed mechanisms to maintain solidarity and undertake political action. These mechanisms can be subsumed under the term *da'wah*, the same word that had been used for the movement that brought the 'Abbasids to power. The *da'wah*'s ability to communicate rapidly over a large area rested on its traveling operatives as well as on a network of local cells. In the late 9th century an Isma'ili movement, nicknamed the Qaramitah (Qarmatians), had seriously but unsuccessfully threatened the 'Abbasids in Syria, Iraq, and Bahrain. Seeking other outlets, a Yemeni operative known as Abu 'Abd Allah al-Shi'i made contact, on the occasion of the *hajj*, with representatives of an Amazigh tribe that had a history of Kharijite hostility to caliphal control. The *hajj* had already become a major vehicle for tying Islamdom's regions together, and Abu 'Abd Allah's movement was only one of many in the Maghrib that would be inaugurated thereby.

In 901 Abu 'Abd Allah arrived in Little Kabylia (in present-day Algeria). For eight years he prepared for an imam, preaching of a millennial restoration of justice after an era of foreign oppression. After conquering the Aghlabid capital al-Qayrawan (in present-day Tunisia), he helped free from a Sijilmassa prison his imam, 'Ubayd Allah, who declared himself the *mahdi*, using a multivalent word that could have quite different meanings for different constituencies. Some Muslims applied *mahdi* to any justice-restoring divinely guided figure; others, including many Jama'i-Sunnis, to the apocalyptic figure expected to usher in the millennium before the Last Judgment; and still others, including most Shi'ites, to a returned or restored imam. Abu 'Abd Allah's followers may have differed in their expectations, but the *mahdi* himself was unequivocal: he was a descendant of 'Ali and Fatimah through Isma'il's disappeared son and therefore was a continuation of the line of the true imam. He symbolized his victory by founding a new capital named, after himself, al-Mahdiyyah (in present-day Tunisia). During the next half century the "Fatimids" tried with limited success to expand westward into the Maghrib and north into the Mediterranean, where they made Sicily a naval base (912–913); but their major goal was Egypt, nominally under 'Abbasid control. From Egypt they would challenge the 'Abbasid caliphate itself. In 969 the Fatimid army conquered the Nile valley and advanced into Palestine and southern Syria as well.

EGYPT, SYRIA, AND THE HOLY CITIES

THE FATIMID DYNASTY

The Fatimids established a new and glorious city, Al-Qahirah ("The Victorious"; Cairo), to rival 'Abbasid Baghdad. They then adopted the title of caliph, laying claim to be the legitimate rulers of all Muslims as well as head of all Isma'ilis. Now three caliphs reigned in Islamdom, where there was supposed to be only one. In Cairo the Fatimids founded a great mosque-school complex, al-Azhar. They fostered local handicraft production and revitalized the Red Sea route from India to the Mediterranean. They built up a navy to trade as well as to challenge the Byzantines and underscore the 'Abbasid caliph's failure to defend and extend the frontiers. Fatimid occupation of the holy cities of Mecca and Medina, complete by the end of the 10th century, had economic as well as spiritual significance: it reinforced the caliph's claim to leadership of all Muslims, provided wealth, and helped him keep watch on the west Arabian coast, from the Hejaz to the Yemen, where a sympathetic Zaydi Shi'ite dynasty had ruled since 897. Fatimid presence in the Indian Ocean was even strong enough to establish an Isma'ili missionary in Sind. The Fatimids patronized the arts; Fatimid glass and ceramics were some of Islamdom's most brilliant. As in other regions, imported styles and tastes were transformed by or supplemented with local artistic impulses, especially in architecture, the most characteristic form of Islamicate art.

The reign of one of the most unusual Fatimid caliphs, al-Hakim, from 996 to 1021, again demonstrated the interregional character of the Isma'ili movement. Historians describe al-Hakim's personal habits as eccentric,

AL-AZHAR UNIVERSITY

Al-Azhar University (Arabic: Jami'at al-Azhar) is a chief locus of Islamic and Arabic learning centred on the mosque of that name in the medieval quarter of Cairo. It was founded by the Shi'ite (specifically, the Isma'ili sect) Fatimids in 970 CE and was formally organized by 988. Its name may allude to Fatimah, the Prophet's daughter, known as "al-Zahra'" ("the Luminous"), from whom the Fatimid dynasty derives its name. The format of education at al-Azhar remained relatively informal for much of its early history: initially there were no entrance requirements, no formal curriculum, and no degrees. The basic program of studies was—and still is—Islamic law, theology, and the Arabic language.

An Isma'ili centre of learning, al-Azhar fell into eclipse after Egypt's conquer by Saladin, founder of the Ayyubid dynasty and a Sunni, in the second half of the 12th century. It was revived under the Mamluks (1250–1517), however, and continued to thrive thereafter as a centre of Sunni scholarship. It was damaged in an earthquake in the early 1300s and subsequently repaired, and additions, alterations, and renovations to its structures were undertaken at various points throughout the 14th and 15th centuries,

Muslim worshippers wait to begin Friday prayers at the al-Azhar mosque in Cairo, Egypt. Marwan Naamani/AFP/Getty Images

particularly in the later Mamluk period, when it came under direct patronage.

With the defeat of the Mamluks in 1517, substantial architectural projects were few until the mid-18th century. In spite of this, al-Azhar's significance continued, and under Ottoman rule it held preeminent status among Egyptian institutions of learning. Opposition to the French in the late 18th century led to an uprising in 1798 centred on al-Azhar, and as a result it was bombarded by the French and temporarily closed. Nineteenth-century reform at al-Azhar owed in part to the involvement of a number of individuals. These included Jamal al-Din al-Afghani, who taught at al-Azhar in the 1870s and emphasized that modern science and other subjects were not incompatible with the Qur'an, and Muhammad 'Abduh, who was influenced as a young intellectual by al-Afghani and later proposed, as a member of a government committee, a number of broad measures for reforming al-Azhar. In the late 19th century, procedures, including admission requirements and examinations, were formalized, and a number of modern subjects—some of them obligatory—were introduced.

Al-Azhar was nationalized and again underwent substantial reforms in the early 1960s. Since that time, faculties such as those of medicine and engineering have been established; women were first admitted in 1962. The modern university offers a number of faculties, some of them for women, as well as regional facilities.

mercurial, and unpredictable to the point of cruelty and his religious values as inconsistent with official Isma'ili teachings, tending toward some kind of accommodation with the Jama'i-Sunni majority. After he vanished under mysterious circumstances, his religious revisionism was not pursued by his successors or by the Isma'ili establishment in Egypt, but in Syria it inspired a peasant revolt that produced the Druze, who still await al-Hakim's return.

THE HAMDANID DYNASTY

When the Fatimids expanded into southern Syria, another Shiʻite dynasty, the Hamdanids, of Bedouin origin, had been ruling northern Syria from Mosul since 905. In 944 a branch of the family had taken Aleppo. Under the leadership of their most famous member, Sayf al-Dawlah (ruled *c.* 943–967), the Hamdanids responded aggressively to renewed Byzantine expansionism in eastern Anatolia. They ruled from Aleppo until they were absorbed by the Fatimids after 1004; at their court some of Islamdom's most lastingly illustrious writers found patronage. Two notable examples are the poet al-Mutanabbi (915–965), who illustrated the importance of the poet as a premodern press agent of the court, and al-Farabi, who tried to reconcile reason and revelation.

Al-Farabi contributed to the ongoing Islamization of Hellenistic thought. *Falsafah*, the Arabic cognate for the Greek *philosophia*, included metaphysics and logic, as well as the positive sciences, such as mathematics, music, astronomy, and anatomy. *Faylasuf*s often earned their living as physicians, astrologers, or musicians. The *faylasuf*'s whole way of life, like that of the *adib*, reflected his studies. It was often competitive with that of more self-consciously observant Muslims because the *faylasuf* often questioned the relationship of revelation to real truth. The *faylasuf*s felt free to explore inner truths not exposed to the view of ordinary people; they practiced prudent concealment (*taqiyyah*) of their deeper awareness wherever making it public might endanger the social order. The *faylasuf*s shared the principle of concealment with the Shiʻites; both believed, for rather different reasons, that inner truth was accessible to only a very few. This esotericism had counterparts in all premodern societies, where learning and literacy were severely restricted.

IRAQ

Cultural Flowering in Iraq

By the late 9th and early 10th centuries the last remnant of the caliphal state was Iraq, under control of the Turkic soldiery. Political decline and instability did not preclude cultural creativity and productivity, however. In fact, Iraq's "generation of 870," loosely construed, contained some of the most striking and lastingly important figures in all of early Islamicate civilization. Three of them illustrate well the range of culture in late 9th- and early 10th-century Iraq: the historian and Qur'anic exegete al-Tabari (*c.* 839–923), the theologian Abu al-Hasan al-Ash'ari (*c.* 873–*c.* 935), and the ecstatic mystic al-Hallaj (*c.* 858–922).

Al-Tabari was born in Tabaristan, south of the Caspian Sea, and as a young man he traveled to Baghdad. Rarely could a man earn his living from religious learning; unless he found patronage, he would probably engage in trade or a craft. All the more astounding was the productivity of scholars like al-Tabari, who said that he produced 40 leaves a day for 40 years. The size of his extant works, which include a commentary on the Qur'an and a universal history, testifies to the accuracy of his claim. His history is unique in sheer size and detail and especially in its long-term impact. His method involved the careful selection, organization, and juxtaposition of separate and often contradictory accounts cast in the form of Hadith. This technique celebrated the *ummah*'s collective memory and established a range of acceptable disagreement.

Al-Ash'ari, from Basra, made his contribution to systematic theological discourse (*kalam*). He had been attracted early to a leading Mu'tazilite teacher, but he broke away at the age of 40. He went on to use Mu'tazilite methods of reasoning to defend popular ideas such as the eternality and literal truth of the Qur'an and the centrality of Muhammad's Sunnah as conveyed by Hadith. Where his approach yielded objectionable results, such as an anthropomorphic rendering of God or a potentially

AL-TABARI

As a youth, Abu Ja'far Muhammad ibn Jarir al-Tabari (c. 839–923) demonstrated a precocious intellect and journeyed from his native town to study in the major centres of learning in Iraq, Syria, and Egypt. Over the course of many years he collected oral and written material from numerous scholars and libraries for his later work. Al-Tabari enjoyed sufficient financial independence to enable him to devote the latter part of his life to teaching and writing in Baghdad, the capital of the 'Abbasid caliphate, where he died in 923. The times in which he lived were marked by political disorder, social crisis, and philosophical-theological controversy. Discontent of diverse cause and circumstance brought open rebellion to the very heart of the caliph's empire, and, like all movements of socioeconomic origin in medieval Islam, sought legitimacy in religious expression directed against the official credo of Sunni orthodoxy.

Al-Tabari rejected out of hand the extreme theological positions of these opposition movements, but at the same time he also retreated from the embrace of the ultraorthodox Sunni faction, the Hanbali (a major school of Islamic law), which was represented most powerfully in the capital itself. An independent within orthodox ranks, he established his own school of jurisprudence, which did not long survive his own death. He nevertheless made a distinct contribution to the consolidation of Sunni thought during the 9th century. What al-Tabari accomplished for historical and Qur'anic studies consisted less in the discovery and initial recording of material than in the sifting and reorganization of it. His achievement was to condense the vast wealth of exegetical and historical erudition of the preceding generations of Muslim scholars (many of whose works are not extant in their original form) and to lay the foundations for both Qur'anic and historical sciences.

In his *Qur'an Commentary*, al-Tabari's method of composition was to follow the Qur'an text word by word, juxtaposing all of the juridical, lexicographical, and historical explanations transmitted in reports from the Prophet Muhammad, his companions, and their followers. To each report (hadith) was affixed a chain of "transmitters" (*isnad*) purporting to go back to the original informant. Divergent reports were seldom reconciled, the scholar's only critical tool being his judgment as to the soundness of the *isnad* and not of the content of the Hadith. Thus plurality of interpretation was admitted on principle.

The popular *History of Prophets and Kings*—which followed the *Commentary*—commenced with the Creation, followed by accounts regarding the patriarchs, prophets, and rulers of antiquity. The history of the Sasanian kings came next. For the period of the Prophet's life, al-Tabari drew upon the extensive researches of 8th-century Medinan scholars. Although pre-Islamic influences are evident in their works, the Medinan perspective of Muslim history evolved as a theocentric (god-centred) universal history of prophecy culminating in the career of Muhammad and not as a continuum of tribal wars and values.

The sources for al-Tabari's *History* covering the years from the Prophet's death to the fall of the Umayyad dynasty (661–750 CE) were short monographs, each treating a major event or the circumstances attending the death of an important person. Al-Tabari supplemented this material with historical reports embodied in works on genealogy, poetry, and tribal affairs. Further, details of the early 'Abbasid period were available to him in a few histories of the caliphs that unfortunately have come down only in the fragments preserved by al-Tabari. Almost all of these accounts reflected an Iraqi perspective of the community; coupled with this is al-Tabari's scant attention to affairs in Egypt, North Africa, and Muslim Spain, so that his *History* does not have the secular "universal" outlook sometimes attributed to it. From the beginning of the Muslim era (dated from 622, the date of the Hijrah—the Prophet Muhammad's migration from Mecca to Medina), the *History* is arranged as a set of annals according to the years after the Hijrah. It terminates in the year 915.

Obviously, al-Tabari could not sustain his preference for reports originating with the Prophet and the pious scholars of the early community known as *al-salaf*. His judgment of a report's reliability was now based upon the largely theoretical criterion that it should originate with either an eyewitness or a contemporary informant. This posed a problem for which al-Tabari had no practical solution. Oftentimes he placed separate accounts of an event side by side without editorial comment. He saw no relevance in searching for the nature and causes of events, for any ultimate explanation lay beyond history itself and was known to God alone. Prophetic tradition, like the Qur'an, provided positive commands and injunctions from God. History pointed to the consequences of heeding or ignoring him. For al-Tabari, therefore, history was the divine will teaching by example.

polytheistic understanding of his attributes, al-Ash'ari resorted to the principle of *bila kayf* ("without regard to the how"), whereby a person of faith accepts that certain fundamentals are true without regard to how they are true and that divine intention is not always accessible to human intelligence. Al-Ash'ari's harmonization also produced a simple creed, which expressed faith in God, his angels, and his books, and affirmed belief in Muhammad as God's last messenger and in the reality of death, physical resurrection, the Last Judgment, and heaven and hell. Taken together, al-Tabari's historiography and al-Ash'ari's theology symbolize the consolidation of Jama'i-Sunni, Shari'ah-minded thought and piety.

The most visible and powerful 10th-century exponent of Sufism was al-Hallaj. By his day, Sufism had grown far beyond its early forms, which were represented by al-Hasan al-Basri (died 728), who practiced *zuhd*, or rejection of the world, and by Rabi'ah al-'Adawiyyah (died 801), who formulated the Sufi ideal of a disinterested love of God. The mystics Abu Yazid Bistami (died 874) and Abu al-Qasim al-Junayd (died 910) had begun to pursue the experience of unity with God, first by being "drunk" with his love and with love of him and then by acquiring life-transforming self-possession and control. Masters (called sheikhs or *pirs*) were beginning to attract disciples (*murids*) to their way. Like other Muslims who tried to go "beyond" the Shari'ah to inner truth, the Sufis practiced conceal-ment of inner awareness (*taqiyyah*). Al-Hallaj, one of al-Junayd's disciples, began to travel and preach publicly, however. His success was disturbing enough for the authorities in Baghdad to have him arrested and con-demned to death; he was tortured and beheaded, and finally his body was burned. Yet his career had shown the power of Sufism, which would by the 12th century become an institutionalized form of Islamic piety.

THE BUYID DYNASTY

Long before, however, a major political change occurred at Baghdad. In 945 control over the caliphs passed from their Turkish soldiery to a dynasty known as the Buyids or Buwayhids. The Buyids came from Daylam, near the southern coast of the Caspian Sea. Living beyond the reach of the caliphs in Baghdad, its residents had identified with Imami Shi'ism. By about 930 three sons of a fisherman named Buyeh had emerged as leaders in Daylam. One of them conquered Baghdad, not replacing the caliph but ruling in his name. The fact that they were Shi'ite, as were the Idrisids, Fatimids, and Hamdanids, led scholars to refer to the period from the mid-10th to mid-11th century as the Shi'ite century.

Like other contemporary rulers, the Buyids were patrons of culture, especially of speculative thought (Shi'ism, Mu'tazilism, *kalam*, and *falsafah*). Jama'i-Sunni learning continued to be patronized by the caliphs and their families. The Buyids favoured no one party over another. However, their openness paradoxically invited a hardening in Jama'i-Sunni thought. Buyid attempts to maintain the cultural brilliance of the court at Baghdad were limited by a decline in revenue occasioned partly by a shift in trade routes to Fatimid Egypt, and partly by long-term neglect of Iraq's irrigation works. The caliphs had occasionally made land assignments (*t*) to soldiers in lieu of paying salaries; now the Buyids extended the practice to other individuals and thus removed an important source of revenue from central control. After 983, Buyid territories were split among various members of the family, and pressure was applied to their borders from both the west (by Hamdanids and Fatimids) and the east (by Samanids, Ghaznavids, and Seljuqs).

The economic difficulties of Buyid Iraq promoted urban unrest, accounts of which provide a rare glimpse into the lives of ordinary Muslim town dwellers. Numerous movements served as outlets for socioeconomic grievances, directed most often toward the wealthy or the military. The concentration of wealth in the cities had produced a bipolar stratification system conveyed in the sources by a pair of words, *khass* (special) and *'amm* (ordinary). In the environment of 10th- and 11th-century Iraq, an instance of rising food prices or official maltreatment could easily spark riots of varying size, duration, and intensity. Strategies for protest included raiding, looting, and assault. Some movements were more coherently ideological than others, and various forms of piety could reflect socioeconomic distinctions. Some movements were particularly attractive to artisans, servants, and soldiers, as was the case with the proponents of Hadith, whose mentor, Ahmad ibn Hanbal (died 855), was viewed as a martyr because of his suffering at the hands of the caliph. Other forms of piety, such as Shi'ism, could be associated with wealthier elements among the landowning and merchant classes.

Beneath the more organized forms of social action lay a more fluid kind of association, most often described by the labels 'ayyar and futuwwah. These terms refer to individuals acting in concert, as needed, on the basis of certain rough-hewn concepts of proper male public behaviour. Such associations had counterparts in the late Hellenistic world, just as they have parallels in the voluntary protective associations formed in the 19th and 20th centuries whenever official institutions of protection were either chronically or temporarily deficient. For some of the Islamicate "gangs" or "clubs," thuggery may have been the norm; for others, the figure of the fourth caliph and first imam, 'Ali, seems to have provided an exemplar. Even though Shi'ites had become a separate group with a distinctive interpretation of 'Ali's significance, a more generalized affection for the family of the Prophet and especially for 'Ali was widespread among Jama'i-Sunnis. 'Ali had come to be recognized as the archetypal young male (fata). A related word, futuwwah, signified groups of young men who pursued such virtues as courage, aiding the weak, generosity, endurance of suffering, love of truth, and hospitality.

Premodern Islamicate societies were characterized by a high degree of fluidity, occasionalism, and voluntarism in the structuring of associations, organizations, loyalties, and occupations. Although all societies must develop ways to maintain social boundaries, ease interaction among groups, and buffer friction, the ways in which Muslim societies have fulfilled these needs seem unusually diffi-cult to delineate. For example, in Muslim cities of the period under discussion, the only official officeholders were appointees of the central government, such as the governor; the *muhtasib*, a transformed Byzantine *agorano-mos* who was monitor of public morality as well as of fair-market practice; or the *sahib al-shurtah*, head of the police. In the absence of an organized church or ordained clergy, those whose influence derived from piety or learn-ing were influential because they were recognized as such, not because they were appointed, and men of very differ-ent degrees of learning might earn the designation of *'alim*. Although the ruler was expected to contribute to the maintenance of public services, neither he nor anyone else was obligated to do so. Though the ruler might maintain prisons for those whose behaviour he disapproved, the local *qadi*s had need of none, relying generally on persua-sion or negotiation and borrowing the caliphal police on the relatively rare occasion on which someone needed to be brought before them by force. There was no formalized mode of succession for any of the dynasties of the time. Competition, sometimes armed, was relied upon to pro-duce the most qualified candidate.

Patronage was an important basis of social organiza-tion. The family served as a premodern welfare agency; where it was absent, minimal public institutions, such as hospitals, provided. One of the most important funding mechanisms for public services was a private one, the *waqf*. The *waqf* provided a legal way to circumvent the Shari'ah's requirement that an individual's estate be divided among many heirs. Through a *waqf*, an individual could endow an institution or group with all or part of his estate, in per-petuity, before his death. A *waqf* might provide books for a school, candles or mats for a mosque, salaries of religious functionaries, or land for a hospital or caravansary. *Waqf*

money or lands were indivisible, although they might contribute to the welfare of a potential heir who happened to
be involved in the *waqf*-supported activity. The *waqf*, like
other forms of patronage, provided needed social services
without official intervention. On other occasions, wealthy
individuals, especially those connected with the ruling
family, might simply patronize favourite activities. In addition to patronage, many other overlapping ties bound
individual Muslims together: loyalties to an occupation—
soldier, merchant, learned man, artisan, government
worker—and loyalties to a town or neighbourhood, or to
a form of piety, or to persons to whom one made an oath
for a specific purpose; and ties to patron or to family,
especially foster-parentage (*istina'*), the counterpart of
which was significant in medieval Christendom.

The Qur'an and Shari'ah discouraged corporate
responsibility in favour of individual action; even the legal
scope of partnership was limited. Yet the unstable political realities that had militated against the emergence of
broad-based institutions sometimes called for corporate
action, as when a city came to terms with a new ruler or
invader. In those cases, a vaguely defined group of notables,
known usually as *a'yan*, might come together to represent
their city in negotiations, only to cease corporate action
when the more functional small-group loyalties could
safely be resumed. Within this shifting frame of individuals
and groups, the ruler was expected to maintain a workable,
if not equitable, balance. More often than not the real
ruler was a local *amir* of some sort. For this reason, the de
facto system of rule that emerged during this period,
despite the persistence of the central caliphate in Baghdad,
has sometimes been referred to as the *a'yan-amir* system.

The city's physical and social organization reflected
this complex relationship between public and private and

between individual and group. It was marked by physically separated quarters; multiple markets and mosques; maze-like patterns of narrow streets and alleys with dwellings oriented toward an inner courtyard; an absence of public meeting places other than bath, market, and mosque; and the concentration of social life in private residences. The *qadi* and *adib* al-Tanukhi provides a lively and humorous picture of 10th-century Baghdad, of a society of individuals with overlapping affiliations and shifting statuses: saints and scoundrels, heroes and rogues, rich men and poor. This mobility is illustrated by al-Tanukhi's boast to a rival, "My line begins with me while yours ends with you." The prose genre of *maqamah*, said to have been invented by al-Hamadhani (died 1008), recounted the exploits of a clever, articulate scoundrel dependent on his own wits for his survival and success.

IRAN, AFGHANISTAN, AND INDIA

In the middle of the "Shi'ite century" a major Sunni revival occurred in eastern Islamdom in connection with the emergence of the second major language of Islamicate high culture, New Persian. This double revival was accomplished by two Iranian dynasties, the Samanids and the Ghaznavids; Ghaznavid zeal even spilled over into India.

THE SAMANIDS

The Samanid dynasty (819–999) stemmed from a local family appointed by the 'Abbasids to govern at Bukhara and Samarkand. Gradually the Samanids had absorbed the domains of the rebellious Tahirids and Saffarids in north-eastern Iran and reduced the Saffarids to a small state in Sistan. The Samanids, relying on Turkic slave troops, also managed to contain the migratory pastoralist Turkic tribes who continually pressed on Iran from across the Oxus River. In the 950s they even managed to convert some of these Turkic tribes to Islam.

The Samanid court at Bukhara attracted leading scholars, such as the philosophers Abu Bakr al-Razi (died 925 or 935) and Avicenna (Ibn Sina; 980–1037), who later worked for the Buyids; and the poet Ferdowsi (died *c.* 1020). Though not Shi'ites, the Samanids expressed an interest in Shi'ite thought, especially in its Isma'ili form, which was then the locus of so much intellectual vitality. The Samanids also fostered the development of a second Islamicate language of high culture, New Persian. It combined the grammatical structure and vocabulary of spoken Persian with vocabulary from Arabic, the existing language of high culture in Iran. A landmark of this "Persianizing" of Iran was Ferdowsi's epic poem, the *Shah-nameh* ("Book of Kings"), written entirely in New Persian in a long-couplet form (*masnavi*) derived from Arabic. Covering several thousand years of detailed mythic Iranian history, Ferdowsi brought Iran's ancient heroic lore, and its hero Rustam, into Islamicate literature and into the identity of self-consciously Iranian Muslims. He began to compose the poem under the rule of the Samanids; but he dedicated the finished work to a dynasty that had meanwhile replaced them, the Ghaznavids.

THE GHAZNAVIDS

The Ghaznavid dynasty was born in a way that had become routine for Islamicate polities. Sebüktigin (ruled 977–997), a Samanid Turkic slave governor in Ghazna (now Ghazni), in the Afghan mountains, made himself independent of his masters as their central power declined. His eldest son, Mahmud, expanded into Buyid territory in western Iran,

The city of Bukhara in modern Uzbekistan. In the foreground is the Mir-e 'Arab Madrasa, an educational institution. Christopher Herwig/Aurora/ Getty Images

identifying himself staunchly with Sunni Islam. Presenting himself as a frontier warrior against the pagans, Mahmud invaded and plundered northwestern India, establishing a permanent rule in the Punjab, but it was through ruling Iran, which gave a Muslim ruler true prestige, that Mahmud sought to establish himself. He declared his loyalty to the 'Abbasid caliph, whose "investiture" he sought, and expressed his intention to defend Sunni Islam against the Shi'ite Buyids. Although he and his regime were proud of their Turkic descent, Mahmud encouraged the use of New Persian, with its echoes of pre-Islamic Iranian glory, for administration and for prose as well as poetry. This combination of Turkic identity and Persian language would characterize and empower many other Muslim rulers.

To Ghazna Mahmud brought, sometimes by force, writers and artisans who could adorn his court. Among these was al-Biruni (973–c. 1050), whose scholarly achievements no contemporary could rival. Before being brought to Ghazna, al-Biruni had served the Samanids and the Khwarazm-Shahs, a local dynasty situated just west of the Oxus River. Al-Biruni's works included studies of astronomy (he even suggested a heliocentric universe), gems, drugs, mathematics, and physics, but his most famous book, inspired by accompanying Mahmud on his Indian campaigns, was a survey of Indian life, language, religion, and culture.

Like most other rulers of the day, Mahmud styled himself an emir and emphasized his loyalty to the caliph in Baghdad, but he and later Ghaznavid rulers also called themselves by the Arabic word *sultan*. Over the next five centuries the office of sultan would become an alternative to caliph. The Ghaznavid state presaged other changes as well, especially by stressing the cleavage between ruler and ruled and by drawing into the ruling class not only the military but also the bureaucracy and the learned establishment. So tied was the ruling establishment to the ruler that it even moved with him on campaign. Ghaznavid "political theory" shared with other states the concept of the circle of justice or circle of power—i.e., that justice is best preserved by an absolute monarch completely outside society; that such a ruler needs an absolutely loyal army; and that maintaining such an army requires prosperity, which in turn depends on the good management of an absolute ruler.

Abu al-Fadl Bayhaqi (995–1077) worked in the Ghaznavid chancery and wrote a remarkable history of the Ghaznavids, the first major prose work in New Persian. He exhibited the broad learning of even a relatively minor figure at court; in his history he combined the effective writing skills of the chancery employee, the special knowledge of Qur'an and Hadith, and the sophisticated and entertaining literature—history, poetry, and folklore—that characterized the *adib*. He provided a vivid picture of life at court, graphically portraying the pitfalls of military absolutism—the dependence of the monarch on a fractious military and a large circle of assistants and advisors, who could mislead him and affect his decision making through internecine maneuvering and competition. In the reign of Mahmud's son, Mas'ud I, the weaknesses in the system had already become glaringly apparent. At the Battle of Dandanqan (1040), Mas'ud lost control of Khorasan, his main holding in Iran, to the pastoralist Seljuq Turks. He then decided to withdraw to Lahore in his Indian domains, from which his successors ruled until overtaken by the Ghurids in 1186.

THE DECLINE OF THE CALIPHATE AND RISE OF EMIRATES

By the end of Mas'ud's reign, government in Islamdom had become government by emir. Caliphal centralization had lasted 200 years; even after the caliphal empire became too large and complex to be ruled from a single centre, the separate emirates that replaced it all defined their legitimacy in relation to it, for or against. In fact, the caliphate's first systematic description and justification was undertaken just when its impracticality was being demonstrated. As the Ghaznavids were ruling in Iran as "appointed" defenders of the caliph, a Baghdadi legal scholar named al-Mawardi (died 1058) retrospectively delineated the minimal requirements of the caliphate and tried to explain why it had become necessary for caliphal powers to be "delegated" in order for the *ummah*'s security to be maintained. Whereas earlier legists had tied the caliph's legitimacy to his defense of the borders, al-Mawardi separated the two, maintaining the caliph as the ultimate source of legitimacy and the guardian of pan-Islamic concerns and relegating day-to-day government to his "appointees." Al-Mawardi may have hoped that the Ghaznavids would expand far enough to be "invited" by the caliph to replace the uninvited Shi'ite Buyids. This replacement did occur, three years before al-Mawardi's death; however, it was not the Ghaznavids who appeared in Baghdad but rather the migratory pastoralist Turks who had meanwhile replaced them. The Seljuqs joined many other migrating groups to produce the next phase of Islamicate history.

CHAPTER 5

MIGRATION AND RENEWAL (1041–1405)

During this period, migrating peoples once again played a major role, perhaps greater than that of the Arabs during the 7th and 8th centuries. No other civilization in premodern history experienced so much in-migration, especially of alien and disruptive peoples, or showed a greater ability to assimilate as well as to learn from outsiders. Nowhere has the capacity of a culture to redefine and incorporate the strange and the foreign been more evident. In this period, which ends with the death in 1405 of Timur (Tamerlane), the last great tribal conqueror, the tense yet creative relationship between sedentary and migratory peoples emerged as one of the great themes of Islamicate history, played out as it was in the centre of the great arid zone of Eurasia. Because this period can be seen as the history of peoples as well as of regions, and because the mobility of those peoples brought them to more than one cultural region, this period should be treated group by group rather than region by region.

As a general term, "migrating" peoples is preferable because it does not imply aimlessness, as "nomadic" does;

or herding, as "pastoralist" does; or kin-related, as "tribal" does. "Migrating" focuses simply on movement from one home to another. Although the Franks, as the Crusaders are called in Muslim sources, differed from other migrating peoples, most of whom were pastoralists related by kinship, they too were migrating warriors organized to invade and occupy peoples to whom they were hostile and alien. Though not literally tribal, they appeared to behave like a tribe with a distinctive way of life and a solidarity based on common values, language, and objectives. Viewing them as alien immigrants comparable to, say, the Mongols helps to explain their reception: how they came to be assimilated into the local culture and drawn into the intra-Muslim factional competition and fighting that was under way in Syria when they arrived.

TURKS

For almost 400 years a succession of Turkic peoples entered eastern Islamdom from Central Asia. These nearly continuous migrations can be divided into three phases: Seljuqs (1055–92), Mongols (1256–1411), and neo-Mongols (1369–1405). Their long-term impact, more constructive than destructive on balance, can still be felt through the lingering heritage of the great Muslim empires they inspired. The addition of tribally organized warrior Turks to the already widely used Turkic slave soldiery gave a single ethnic group an extensive role in widening the gap between rulers and ruled.

SELJUQ TURKS

The Seljuqs were a family among the Oghuz Turks, a label applied to the migratory pastoralists of the Syr Darya–Oxus

Fourteenth-century vellum depicting the sultan Alp-Arslan, the second ruler of the Seljuq dynasty. Ms Or 20 f.138r/Edinburgh University Library, Scotland/With kind permission of the University of Edinburgh/The Bridgeman Art Library

basin. Their name has come to stand for the group of Oghuz families led into Ghaznavid Khorasan after they had been converted to Sunni Islam, probably by Sufi missionaries after the beginning of the 11th century. In 1040 the Seljuqs' defeat of the Ghaznavid sultan allowed them to proclaim themselves rulers of Khorasan. Having expanded into western Iran as well, Toghrïl Beg, also using the title "sultan," was able to occupy Baghdad (1055) after "petitioning" the 'Abbasid caliph for permission. The Seljuqs quickly took the remaining Buyid territory and began to occupy Syria, whereupon they encountered Byzantine resistance in the Armenian highlands. In 1071 a Seljuq army under Alp-Arslan defeated the Byzantines at Manzikert north of Lake Van; while the main Seljuq army replaced the Fatimids in Syria, large independent tribal bands occupied Anatolia, coming closer to the Byzantine capital than had any other Muslim force.

POLICIES OF NIZAM AL-MULK

The Seljuqs derived their legitimacy from investiture by the caliph, and from "helping" him reunite the *ummah*; yet their governing style prefigured the emergence of true alternatives to the caliphate. Some of their Iranian advisers urged them to restore centralized absolutism as it had existed in pre-Islamic times and in the period of Marwanid-'Abbasid strength. The best-known proponent was Nizam al-Mulk, chief minister to the second and third Seljuq sultans, Alp-Arslan and Malik-Shah. Nizam al-Mulk explained his plans in his *Seyasat-nameh* (*The Book of Government*), one of the best-known manuals of Islamicate political theory and administration. He was unable, however, to persuade the Seljuq sultans to assert enough power over other tribal leaders. Eventually the Seljuq sultans, like so many rulers before them, alienated their tribal supporters and resorted to the costly alternative of a Turkic slave core, whose leading members were appointed to tutor and train young princes of the Seljuq family to compete for rule on the death of the reigning sultan. The tutors were known as *atabeg*s. More often than not, they became the actual rulers of the domains assigned to their young charges, cooperating with urban notables (*a'yan*) in day-to-day administration.

Although Nizam al-Mulk was not immediately successful, he did contribute to long-term change. He encouraged the establishment of state-supported schools (madrasahs); those he personally patronized were called Nizamiyyahs. The most important Nizamiyyah was founded in Baghdad in 1067. There Nizam al-Mulk gave government stipends to teachers and students whom he hoped he could subsequently not only appoint to the position of *qadi* but also recruit for the bureaucracy. Systematic and broad instruction in Jama'i-Sunni learning would counteract the disruptive influences of non-Sunni or anti-Sunni thought and activity, particularly the continuing agitation of Isma'ili Muslims. In 1090 a group of Isma'ilis established themselves in a mountain fortress at Alamut in the mountains of Daylam. From there they began to coordinate revolts all over Seljuq domains. Nominally loyal to the Fatimid caliph in Cairo, the eastern Isma'ilis confirmed their growing independence and radicalism by supporting a failed contender for the Fatimid caliphate, Nizar. For that act they were known as the Nizari Isma'ilis. They were led by Hasan-e Sabbah and were dubbed by their detractors the *hashishiyyin* (assassins) because they practiced political murder while they were allegedly under the influence of hashish.

Nizam al-Mulk's madrasah system enhanced the prestige and solidarity of the Jama'i-Sunni *ulama* without actually drawing them into the bureaucracy or combating anti-Sunni agitation, but it also undermined their autonomy. It established the connection between state-supported education and office holding, and it subordinated the spiritual power and prestige of the *ulama* to the indispensable physical force of the military emirs. Nizam al-Mulk unintentionally encouraged the independence of these emirs by extending the *iqta'* system beyond Buyid practice. He regularly assigned land revenues to individual military officers, assuming that he could keep them under bureaucratic control. When that failed, his system increased the emirs' independence and drained the central treasury.

The madrasah system had other unpredictable results that can be illustrated by al-Ghazali, who was born in 1058

NIZAM AL-MULK

Abu 'Ali Hasan ibn 'Ali ibn Ishaq al-Tusi (1018/19–1092), known as Nizam al-Mulk (Arabic: "Order of the Kingdom"), was the son of a revenue official for the Ghaznavid dynasty. Through his father's position, he was born into the literate, cultured milieu of the Persian administrative class. His early years included a religious education, and he spent significant time with jurists and scholars of religion. In the years of confusion following the initial Seljuq Turk expansion, his father left Tus for Ghazna (now in Afghanistan), where Nizam al-Mulk, too, in due course entered Ghaznavid service.

He soon returned to Khorasan, however, and joined the service of Alp-Arslan, who was then the Seljuq governor there. When Alp-Arslan's vizier died, Nizam al-Mulk was appointed to succeed him, and, when Alp-Arslan himself succeeded his father in 1059, Nizam al-Mulk had the entire administration of Khorasan in his hands. His abilities so pleased his master that, when Alp-Arslan became the supreme overlord of the Seljuq rulers in 1063, Nizam al-Mulk was made vizier.

For the next 30 years, under two remarkable rulers, he occupied this position in an empire that stretched from the Oxus River (now Amu Darya) in the east to Khwarezm and the southern Caucasus and westward into central Anatolia. During these decades, the Seljuq empire was at its zenith; Nizam al-Mulk's influence guided the sultan's decisions, sometimes even military ones, and his firm control of the central and provincial administration, through his numerous dependents and relatives, implemented those decisions. His influence was especially felt in the rule of Sultan Malik-Shah, who succeeded to the Seljuq throne when he was only 18. Such was Nizam al-Mulk's reputation among contemporaries that he was compared to the Barmakids, viziers to the 8th-century caliph Harun al-Rashid.

Shortly before his assassination and at Malik-Shah's request, Nizam al-Mulk wrote down his views on government in the *Seyasat-nameh*. In this remarkable work, he barely refers to the organization of the *dewan* (administration) because he had been able, with the help of his well-chosen servants, to control and model it on traditional lines. But he never had the same power in the *dargah* (court) and found much to criticize in the sultan's careless disregard for protocol, the lack of magnificence in his court, the decline in prestige of important officials, and the neglect of the intelligence service. The most severe criticisms in the *Seyasat-nameh*, however, are of Shi'ite views in general and the Isma'ilis in particular, to whom he devotes his last 11 chapters. His support of "right religion," Sunni Islam, was not only for reasons of state but also a matter of passionate conviction.

Nizam al-Mulk expressed his religious devotion in ways that contributed to the Sunni revival. He founded Nizamiyyah madrasahs in many major towns throughout the empire to combat Shi'ite propaganda, as well as to provide reliable, competent administrators, schooled in his own branch of Islamic law. Less orthodox religious communities among the Sufi orders also benefited from his generosity; hospices, pensions for the poor, and extensive public works related to the pilgrimage to Mecca and Medina were created or sustained by his patronage. Particularly in his last years, when the Isma'ili threat grew stronger and its partisans found a refuge in Alamut, the castle of the Assassins, he set himself the task of combating their influence by every means possible.

On Alp-Arslan's death in 1073, Nizam al-Mulk was left with wider powers, since the late sultan's successor, Malik-Shah, was only a youth. By 1080, however, Malik-Shah had become less acquiescent. Nizam al-Mulk also antagonized the sultan's favourite courtier, Taj al-Mulk, and he made an enemy of the sultan's wife Terken Khatun by preferring the son of another wife for the succession.

Nizam al-Mulk was assassinated in 1092 — a murder that was probably committed by an Isma'ili from Alamut, possibly with the complicity of Taj al-Mulk and Terken Khatun, if not that of Malik-Shah himself. Within a month, however, the sultan too was dead, and the disintegration of the great Seljuq empire had begun.

at Tus and in 1091 was made head of the Baghdad Nizamiyyah. For four years, to great admiration, he taught both *fiqh* and *kalam* and delivered critiques of *falsafah* and Isma'ili thought. According to his autobiographical work *Al-Munqidh min al-dalal* (*The Deliverer from Error*), the more he taught, the more he doubted, until his will and voice became paralyzed. In 1095 he retreated from public life, attempting to arrive at a more satisfying faith. He undertook a radically skeptical reexamination of all of the paths available to the pious Muslim, culminating in an incorporation of the active, immediate, and inspired experience of the Sufis into the Shari'ah-ordered piety of the public cult. For his accomplishments, al-Ghazali was viewed as a renewer (*mujaddid*), a role expected by many Muslims to be filled by at least one figure at the turn of every Muslim century.

TARIQAH FELLOWSHIPS

In the 12th century Muslims began to group themselves into *tariqah*, fellowships organized around and named for the *tariqah* ("way" or "path") of given masters. Al-Ghazali may have had such a following himself. One of the first large-scale orders, the Qadiriyah, formed around the teachings of 'Abd al-Qadir al-Jilani of Baghdad. Though rarely monastic in the European sense, the activities of a *tariqah* often centred around assembly halls (called *khanqah*, *zawiyah*, or *tekke*) that could serve as places of retreat or accommodate special spiritual exercises. The *dhikr*, for example, is a ceremony in which devotees meditated on the name of God to the accompaniment of breathing exercises, music, or movement, so as to attain a state of consciousness productive of a sense of union with God. Although shortcuts and excesses have often made Sufism vulnerable to criticism, its most serious practitioners have conceived of it as a disciplined extension of Shari'ah-minded piety, not an escape. In fact, many Sufis have begun their path through supererogatory fulfillment of standard ritual requirements.

Thousands of *tariqah*s sprang up over the centuries, some associated with particular occupations, locales, or classes. It is possible that by the 18th century most adult Muslim males had some connection with one or more *tariqah*s. The structure of the *tariqah* ensued from the charismatic authority of the master, who, though not a prophet, replicated the direct intimacy that the prophets had shared with God. This quality he passed on to his disciples through a hierarchically ordered network that could extend over thousands of miles. The *tariqah*s thus became powerful centripetal forces among societies in which formal organizations were rare; but the role of the master became controversial because followers often made saints or intercessors of especially powerful Sufi leaders and made shrines or pilgrimage sites of their tombs or birthplaces. Long before these developments could combine to produce stable alternatives to the caliphal system, Seljuq power had begun to decline, only to be replaced for a century and a half with a plethora of small military states. When the Frankish Crusaders arrived in the Holy Land in 1099, no one could prevent them from quickly establishing themselves along the eastern Mediterranean coast.

FRANKS

THE CALL FOR THE CRUSADES

At the Council of Clermont in 1095 Pope Urban II responded to an appeal from the Byzantine emperor for help against the Seljuq Turks, who had expanded into western Anatolia just as the Kipchak Turks in the Ukraine had cut off newly Christian Russia from Byzantium. The First Crusade, begun the next year, brought about the conquest of Jerusalem in 1099. The Christian Reconquista

(Reconquest) of Spain was already under way, having scored its first great victory at Toledo in 1085. Ironically, modern historiography has concentrated on the Crusades that failed and virtually ignored the ones that succeeded. In the four centuries between the fall of Toledo and the fall of Granada (1492), Spanish Christians replaced Muslim rulers throughout the Iberian Peninsula, although Muslims remained as a minority under Christian rule until the early 17th century. In the 200 years from the fall of Jerusalem to the end of the Eighth Crusade (1291), western European Crusaders failed to halt the Turkish advance or to establish a permanent presence in the Holy Land. By 1187 local Muslims had managed to retake Jerusalem and thereby contain Christian ambitions permanently. By the time of the Fourth Crusade (1202–04) the Crusading movement had been turned inward against Christian heretics such as the Byzantines.

EFFECT OF THE CRUSADES IN SYRIA

The direct impact of the Crusades on Islamdom was limited largely to Syria. For the century during which western European Christians were a serious presence there, they were confined to their massive coastal fortifications. The Crusaders had arrived in Syria at one of its most factionalized periods prior to the 20th century. Seljuq control, never strong, was then insignificant; local Muslim rule was anarchic; the Seljuq regime in Baghdad was competing with the Fatimid regime in Egypt; and all parties in Syria were the target of the Nizari Isma'ili movement at Alamut. The Crusaders soon found it difficult to operate as more than just another faction. Yet the significance of the Crusaders as a force against which to be rallied should not be underestimated any more than should the significance of Islamdom as a force against which Christendom could unite.

The Crusaders' situation encouraged interaction with the local population and even assimilation. They needed the food, supplies, and services available in the Muslim towns. Like their Christian counterparts in Spain, they took advantage of the enemy's superior skills, in medicine and hygiene, for example. Because warfare was seasonal and occasional, they spent much of their time in peaceful interaction with their non-Christian counterparts. Some early-generation Crusaders intermarried with Arab Muslims or Arab Christians and adopted their personal habits and tastes, much to the dismay of Christian latecomers. An intriguing account of life in Syria during the Crusades can be found in the *Kitab al-I'tibar* ("Book of Reflection"), the memoirs of Usamah ibn Munqidh (1095–1188). Born in Syria, he was a small boy when the first generation of Franks controlled Jerusalem. As an adult, he fought with Saladin (Salah al-Din Yusuf ibn Ayyub) and lived to see him unite Egypt with Syria and restore Jerusalem to Muslim control. In this fine example of Islamicate autobiographical writing, Usamah draws a picture of the Crusades not easily found in European sources: Christians and Muslims observing, and sometimes admiring, each others' skills and habits, from the battlefield to the bathhouse. Although the Franks in Syria were clearly influenced by the Muslims, the Crusades seem to have contributed relatively little to the overall impact of Islamicate culture on Europe, even though they constituted the most prolonged direct contact.

Although the Crusaders never formed a united front against the Muslims, Syrian Muslims did eventually form a united front against them, largely through the efforts of the family of the emir Zangi, a Turkic slave officer appointed

Painting of the surrender of Richard I before Saladin after the Battle of Hattin in 1187. DEA/G. Dagli Orti/Getty Images

Seljuq representative in Mosul in 1127. After Zangi had extended his control through northern Syria, one of his sons and successors, Nur al-Din (Nureddin), based at Aleppo, was able to tie Zangi's movement to the frontier warrior (*ghazi*) spirit. This he used to draw together urban and military support for a jihad against the Christians. After taking Damascus, he established a second base in Egypt. He offered help to the failing Fatimid regime in return for being allowed to place one of his own lieutenants, Saladin, as chief minister to the Fatimid caliph, thus warding off a Crusader alliance with the Fatimids. This action gave Nur al-Din two fronts from which to counteract the superior seaborne and naval support the Crusaders were receiving from western Europe and the Italian city-states.

SALADIN

Salah al-Din Yusuf ibn Ayyub (1137/38–1193)—known to many in the West as Saladin—was the founder of the Ayyubid dynasty and is among the most famous of Muslim heroes. In wars against the Christian Crusaders, he achieved great success with the capture of Jerusalem (Oct. 2, 1187), ending its nearly nine decades of occupation by the Franks.

Saladin was born into a prominent Kurdish family. His formal career began when he joined the staff of his uncle Asad al-Din Shirkuh, an important military commander under the emir Nur al-Din (the son and successor of 'Imad al-Din Zangi ibn Aq Sonqur, a powerful Turkish governor in northern Syria whom Saladin's father had served). In 1169 at the age of 31, Saladin was appointed both commander of the Syrian troops in Egypt and vizier of the Fatimid caliph there. As vizier of Egypt, he received the title "king" (*malik*), although he was generally known as the sultan.

Saladin's position was further enhanced when, in 1171, he abolished the weak and unpopular Shi'ite Fatimid caliphate, proclaiming a return to Sunni Islam in Egypt. Although he remained for a time theoretically a vassal of Nur al-Din, that relationship ended with the Syrian emir's death in 1174. From 1174 until 1186 he zealously pursued a goal of uniting, under his own standard, all the Muslim territories of Syria, northern Mesopotamia, Palestine, and Egypt. This he accomplished by skillful diplomacy backed when necessary by the swift and resolute use of military force. Gradually his reputation grew as a generous and virtuous but firm ruler, devoid of pretense, licentiousness, and cruelty.

Saladin was able to successfully turn the military balance of power with the Crusaders in his favour—more by uniting and disciplining a great number of unruly forces than by employing new or improved military techniques—and when at last, in 1187, he was able to throw his full strength into the struggle with the Latin Crusader kingdoms, his armies were their equals. On July 4, 1187, aided by his military good sense and by a remarkable lack of it on the part of his enemy, Saladin trapped and destroyed in one blow an exhausted and thirst-crazed army of Crusaders at Hattin, near Tiberias in northern Palestine. So great were the losses in the ranks of the Crusaders in this one battle that the Muslims were quickly able to overrun nearly the entire kingdom of Jerusalem. Acre, Toron, Beirut, Sidon, Nazareth, Caesarea, Nablus, Jaffa (Yafo), and Ascalon (Ashqelon) fell within three months. But Saladin's crowning achievement and the most disastrous blow to the whole Crusading movement came on Oct. 2, 1187, when the city of Jerusalem, holy to both Muslim and Christian alike, surrendered to Saladin's army after 88 years in the hands of the Franks. Saladin planned to avenge the slaughter of Muslims in Jerusalem in 1099 by killing all Christians in the city, but he agreed to let them purchase their freedom provided that the Christian defenders left the Muslim inhabitants unmolested.

His sudden success, which in 1189 saw the Crusaders reduced to the occupation of only three cities, was, however, marred by his failure to capture Tyre, an almost impregnable coastal fortress to which the scattered Christian survivors of the recent battles flocked. It was to be the rallying point of the Latin counterattack. Most probably, Saladin did not anticipate the European reaction to his capture of Jerusalem, an event that deeply shocked the West and to which it responded with a new call for a Crusade. In addition to many great nobles and famous knights, this Crusade, the third, brought the kings of three countries into the struggle. The magnitude of the Christian effort and the lasting impression it made on contemporaries gave the name of Saladin, as their gallant and chivalrous enemy, an added lustre.

The Crusade itself was long and exhausting in spite of the military genius of Richard I (the Lion-Heart). Therein lies the greatest—but often unrecognized—achievement of Saladin. With tired and unwilling feudal levies, committed to fight only a limited season each year, his indomitable will enabled him to fight the greatest champions of Christendom to a draw. The Crusaders retained little more than a precarious foothold on the Levantine coast, and when King Richard left the Middle East, in October 1192, the battle was over. Saladin withdrew to his capital at Damascus, where he died the following year.

Three years before Nur al-Din's death in 1174, Saladin substituted himself for the Fatimid caliph he theoretically served, thus ending more than 200 years of Fatimid rule in Egypt. When Nur al-Din died, Saladin succeeded him as head of the whole movement. When Saladin died in 1193, he had recaptured Jerusalem (1187) and begun the reunification of Egypt and Syria; his successors were known, after his patronymic, as the Ayyubids. The efforts of a contemporary 'Abbasid caliph, al-Nasir, to revive the caliphate seem pale by comparison.

The Ayyubids ruled in Egypt and Syria until around 1250, when they were replaced first in Egypt and later in Syria by the leaders of their own slave-soldier corps, the Mamluks. It was they who expelled the remaining Crusaders from Syria, subdued the remaining Nizari Isma'ilis there, and consolidated Ayyubid holdings into a centralized state. That state became strong enough in its first decade to do what no other Muslim power could: in 1260 at 'Ayn Jalut, south of Damascus, the Mamluk army defeated the recently arrived Mongols and expelled them from Syria.

MONGOLS

The Mongols were pagan, horse-riding tribes of the northeastern steppes of Central Asia. In the early 13th century, under the leadership of Genghis Khan, they formed, led, and gave their name to a confederation of Turkic tribes that they channeled into a movement of global expansion, spreading east into China, north into Russia, and west into Islamdom. Like other migratory peoples before them, Arabs, Imazighen, and Turks, they had come to be involved in citied life through their role in the caravan trade. Unlike others, however, they did not convert to Islam before their arrival. Furthermore, they brought a greater hostility to

GENGHIS KHAN

As far as can be judged from the disparate sources, the personality of the Mongolian warrior-ruler Genghis Khan (1162–1227)—one of the most famous conquerors of history, who consolidated tribes into a unified Mongolia and then extended his empire across Asia to the Adriatic Sea—was a complex one. He had great physical strength, tenacity of purpose, and an unbreakable will. He was not obstinate and would listen to advice from others, including his wives and mother. He was flexible. He could deceive but was not petty. He had a sense of the value of loyalty: enemies guilty of treachery toward their lords could expect short shrift from him, but he would exploit their treachery at the same time. He was religiously minded, carried along by his sense of a divine mission, and in moments of crisis he would reverently worship the Eternal Blue Heaven, the supreme deity of the Mongols.

So much is true of his early life. The picture becomes less harmonious as he moves out of his familiar sphere and comes into contact with the strange, settled world beyond the steppe. At first he could not see beyond the immediate gains to be got from massacre and rapine and, at times, was consumed by a passion for revenge. Yet all his life he could attract the loyalties of men willing to serve him, both fellow nomads and civilized men from the settled world. His fame could even persuade the aged Daoist sage Changchun (Qiu Chuji) to journey the length of Asia to discourse upon religious matters. He was above all adaptable, a man who could learn.

Organization, discipline, mobility, and ruthlessness of purpose were the fundamental factors in his military successes. Massacres of defeated populations, with the resultant terror, were weapons he regularly used. His practice of summoning cities to surrender and of organizing the methodical slaughter of those who did not submit has been described as psychological warfare; but, although it was undoubtedly policy to sap resistance by fostering terror, massacre was used for its own sake. Mongol practice, especially in the war against Khwarezm, was to send agents to demoralize and divide the garrison and populace of an enemy city, mixing threats with promises. The Mongols' reputation for frightfulness often paralyzed their captives, who allowed themselves to be killed when resistance or flight was not impossible. Indeed, the Mongols were unaccountable. Resistance brought certain destruction, but at Balkh, now in Afghanistan, the population was slaughtered in spite of a prompt surrender, for tactical reasons.

The achievements of Genghis Khan were grandiose. He united all the nomadic tribes, and with numerically inferior armies he defeated great empires, such as Khwarezm and the even more powerful Jin state. Yet he did not exhaust his people. He chose his successor, his son Ögödei, with great care, ensured that his other sons would obey Ögödei, and passed on to him an army and a state in full vigour. At the time of his death, Genghis Khan had conquered the landmass extending from Beijing to the Caspian Sea, and his generals had raided Persia and Russia. His successors would extend their power over the whole of China, Persia, and most of Russia. They did what he did not achieve and perhaps never really intended—that is, to weld their conquests into a tightly organized empire. The destruction brought about by Genghis Khan survives in popular memory, but far more significant, these conquests were but the first stage of the Mongol Empire, the greatest continental empire of medieval and modern times.

sedentary civilization, a more ferocious military force, a more cumbersome material culture, a more complicated and hierarchical social structure, and a more coherent sense of tribal law. Their initial impact was physically more destructive than that of previous invaders, and their long-term impact perhaps more socially and politically creative.

First Mongol Incursions

The first Mongol incursions into Islamdom in 1220 were a response to a challenge from the Khwarezm-Shah 'Ala' al-Din Muhammad, the aggressive reigning leader of a dynasty formed in the Oxus Delta by a local governor who had rebelled against the Seljuq regime in Khorasan. Under Genghis Khan's leadership, Mongol forces destroyed numerous cities in Transoxania and Khorasan in an unprecedented display of terror and annihilation. By the time of Genghis Khan's death in 1227, his empire stretched from the Caspian Sea to the Sea of Japan. A later successor, Möngke, decided to extend the empire in two new directions. From the Mongol capital of Karakorum, he simultaneously dispatched Kublai Khan to southern China (where Islam subsequently began to expand inland) and Hülegü to Iran (1256). Hülegü had already received Sunni ambassadors who encouraged him to destroy the Isma'ili state at Alamut. This he did and more, reaching Baghdad in 1258, where he terminated and replaced the caliphate. The 'Abbasid line continued, however, until 1517. The Mamluk sultan Baybars I, shortly after his defeat of the Mongols, invited a member of the 'Abbasid house to "invest" him and to live in Cairo as spiritual head of all Muslims.

The Mongol regimes in Islamdom quickly became rivals. The Il-Khans controlled the Tigris-Euphrates valley and Iran; the Chagatai dominated the Syr Darya and Oxus basins, the Kabul mountains, and eventually the Punjab; and the Golden Horde was concentrated in the Volga basin. The Il-Khans ruled in the territories where Islam was most firmly established. They patronized learning of all types and scholars from all parts of the vast Mongol empire, especially China. Evincing a special interest in nature, they built a major observatory at Maragheh. Just as enthusiastically as they had destroyed citied life, they now rebuilt it, relying as had all previous invaders of Iran on the administrative skills of indigenous Persian-speaking bureaucrats. The writings of one of these men, 'Ata Malek Joveyni, who was appointed governor in Baghdad after the Mongol capture of that city in 1258, described the type of rule the Mongols sought to impose. It has been called the military patronage state because it involved a reciprocal relationship between the foreign tribal military conquerors and their subjects. The entire state was defined as a single mobile military force connected to the household of the monarch; with no fixed capital, it moved with the monarch. All non-Turkic state workers, bureaucratic or religious, even though not military specialists, were defined as part of the army (*asker*); the rest of the subject population, as the herds (*ra'iyyah*). The leading tribal families could dispose of the wealth of the conquered populations as they wished, except that their natural superiority obligated them to reciprocate by patronizing whatever of excellence the cities could produce. What the Ghaznavids and Seljuqs had begun, the Mongols now accomplished. The self-confidence and superiority of the leading families were bolstered by a fairly elaborate set of tribal laws, inherited from Genghis Khan and known as the Yasa, which served to regulate personal status and criminal liability among the Mongol elite, as did the Shari'ah among Muslims. In Il-Khanid hands, this dynastic law merely coexisted but did not compete with Shari'ah; but in later Turkic regimes a reconciliation was achieved that extended the power of the rulers beyond the limitations of an autonomous Shari'ah.

Conversion of Mongols to Islam

For a time the Il-Khans tolerated and patronized all religious persuasions — Sunni, Shi'ite, Buddhist, Nestorian Christian, Jewish, and pagan. But in 1295 a Buddhist named

The Ala'i Gate (left), *built in 1311, and the five-story Qutb Minar, Delhi.*
Frederick M. Asher

Mahmud Ghazan became khan and declared himself Muslim, compelling other Mongol notables to follow suit. His patronage of Islamicate learning fostered such brilliant writers as Rashid al-Din, the physician and scholar who authored one of the most famous Persian universal histories of all time. The Mongols, like other Islamicate dynasties swept into power by a tribal confederation, were able to unify their domains for only a few generations. By the 1330s their rule had begun to be fragmented among myriad local leaders. Meanwhile, on both Mongol flanks, other Turkic Muslim powers were increasing in strength.

To the east the Delhi Sultanate of Turkic slave-soldiers withstood Mongol pressure, benefited from the presence of scholars and administrators fleeing Mongol destruction, and gradually began to extend Muslim control south into India, a feat that was virtually accomplished under Muhammad ibn Tughluq. Muslim Delhi was a culturally lively place that attracted a variety of unusual persons. Muhammad ibn Tughluq himself was, like many later Indian Muslim rulers, well-read in philosophy, science, and religion. Not possessing the kind of dynastic legitimacy the pastoralist Mongols had asserted, he tied his legitimacy to his support for the Shari'ah, and he even sought to have himself invested by the 'Abbasid "caliph" whom the Mamluks had taken to Cairo. His concern with the Shari'ah coincided with the growing popularity of Sufism, especially as represented by the massive Sufi Chishti *tariqah*. Its most famous leader, Nizam al-Din Awliya', had been a spiritual adviser to many figures at court before Muhammad ibn Tughluq came to the throne, as well as to individual Hindus and Muslims alike. In India, Sufism, which inherently undermined communalism, was bringing members of different religious communities together in ways very rare in the more westerly parts of Islamdom.

To the west the similarly constituted Mamluk state continued to resist Mongol expansion. Its sultans were chosen on a nonhereditary basis from among a group of freed slaves who acted as the leaders of the various slave corps. At the death of one sultan, the various military corps would compete to see whose leader would become the next sultan. The leaders of the various slave corps formed an oligarchy that exercised control over the sultan. Although political instability was the frequent and natural result of such a system, cultural florescence did occur. The sultans actively encouraged trade and building, and Mamluk Cairo became a place of splendour, filled with numerous architectural monuments. While the Persian language was becoming the language of administration and high culture over much of Islamdom, Arabic alone continued to be cultivated in Mamluk domains, to the benefit of a diversified intellectual life. Ibn al-Nafis (died 1288), a physician, wrote about pulmonary circulation 300 years before it was "discovered" in Europe. For Mamluk administrative personnel, al-Qalqashandi composed an encyclopaedia in which he surveyed not only local practice but also all the information that a cultivated administrator should know. Ibn Khallikan composed one of the most important Islamicate biographical works, a dictionary of eminent men. Shari'ah-minded studies were elaborated: the *ulama* worked out a political theory that tried to make sense of the sultanate, and they also explored the possibility of enlarging on the Shari'ah by reference to *falsafah* and Sufism.

However, in much the same way as al-Shafi'i had responded in the 9th century to what he viewed as dangerous legal diversity, another great legal and religious reformer, Ibn Taymiyyah, living in Mamluk Damascus in the late 13th and early 14th century, cautioned against such extralegal practices and pursuits. He insisted that the Shari'ah was complete in and of itself and could be adapted to every age by any *faqih* who could analogize according to the principle of human advantage (*maslahah*). A Hanbali himself, Ibn Taymiyyah became as popular as his school's founder, Ahmad ibn Hanbal. Like him, Ibn Taymiyyah attacked all practices that undermined what he felt to be the fundamentals of Islam, including all forms of Shi'ite thought as well as aspects of Jama'i-Sunni piety (often influenced by the Sufis) that stressed knowledge of God over service to him. Most visible among such practices was the revering of saints' tombs, which was condoned by the Mamluk authorities. Ibn Taymiyyah's program and popularity so threatened the Mamluk authorities that they put him in prison, where he died. His movement did not survive, but, when his ideas surfaced in the revolutionary movement of the Wahhabiyyah (Wahhabism) in the late 18th century, their lingering power became dramatically evident.

Farther west, the Rum Seljuqs at Konya submitted to the Mongols in 1243 but survived intact. They continued to cultivate the Islamicate arts, architecture in particular. The most famous Muslim ever to live at Konya, Jalal al-Din Rumi, had emigrated from eastern Iran with his father before the arrival of the Mongols. In Konya, Jalal al-Din, attracted to Sufi activities, attached himself to the master Shams al-Din. The poetry inspired by Jalal al-Din's association with Shams al-Din is unparalleled in Persian literature. Its recitation, along with music and movement, was a key element in the devotional activities of Jalal al-Din's followers, who came to be organized into a Sufi *tariqah*—named the Mevleviyah (Mawlawiyyah) after their title of respect for him, Mevlana ("Our Master"). In his poetry Jalal al-Din explored all varieties of metaphors, including intoxication, to describe the ineffable ecstasy of union with God.

ASCENT OF THE OTTOMAN TURKS

It was not from the Rum Seljuqs, however, that lasting Muslim power in Anatolia was to come, but rather from one of the warrior states on the Byzantine frontier. The successive waves of Turkic migrations had driven unrelated individuals and groups across central Islamdom into Anatolia. Avoiding the Konya state, they gravitated toward an open frontier to the west, where they began to constitute themselves, often through fictitious kinship relationships, into quasi-tribal states that depended on raiding each other and Byzantine territory and shipping. One of these, the Osmanlis, or Ottomans, named for their founder, Osman I (ruled 1281–1324), was located not on the coast, where raiding had its limits, but in Bithynia just facing Constantinople. In the mid-1320s they won the town of Bursa and made it their first capital. From Anatolia they crossed over into Thrace in the service of rival factions at Constantinople, then began to occupy Byzantine territory, establishing their second capital at Edirne on the European side. Their sense of legitimacy was complex. They were militantly Muslim, bound by the *ghazi* spirit, spurred on in their intolerance of local Christians by Greek converts and traveling Sufis who gravitated to their domains. At the same time, *ulama* from more-settled Islamic lands to the east encouraged them to abide by the Shari'ah and tolerate the Christians as protected non-Muslims. The Ottomans also cast themselves as deputies of the Rum Seljuqs, who were themselves originally "deputized" by the 'Abbasid caliph. Finally they claimed descent from the leading Oghuz Turk families, who were natural rulers over sedentary populations. Under Murad I (ruled *c.* 1360–89) the state began to downplay its warrior fervour in favour of more conventional Islamicate administration. Instead of relying on volunteer warriors, Murad established a regular cavalry, which he supported with land assignments, as well as a specially trained infantry force called the "New Troops," Janissaries, drawn from converted captives. Expanding first through western Anatolia and Thrace, the Ottomans under Bayezid I (ruled 1389–1402) turned their eyes toward eastern and southern Anatolia. Just as they had incorporated the whole, they encountered a neo-Mongol conqueror expanding into Anatolia from the east who utterly defeated their entire army in a single campaign (1402).

TIMUR'S EFFORTS TO RESTORE MONGOL POWER

Timur (Tamerlane) was a Turk, not a Mongol, but he aimed to restore Mongol power. He was born a Muslim in the Syr Darya valley and served local pagan Mongol warriors and finally the Chagatai heir apparent, but he rebelled and made himself ruler in Khwarezm in 1380. He planned to restore Mongol supremacy under a thoroughly Islamic program. He surpassed the Mongols in terror, constructing towers out of the heads of his victims. Having established himself in Iran, he moved first on India and then on Ottoman Anatolia and Mamluk Syria, but he died before he could consolidate his realm. His impact was twofold: his defeat of the Ottomans inspired a comeback that would produce one of the greatest Islamicate empires of all time, and one of the Central Asian heirs to his tradition of conquest would found another great Islamicate empire in India. These later empires managed to find the combination of Turkic and Islamic legitimacy that could produce the stable centralized absolutism that had eluded all previous Turkic conquerors.

TIMUR

The Turkic conqueror Timur (1336–1405), remembered for the barbarity of his conquests from India and Russia to the Mediterranean Sea and for the cultural achievements of his dynasty, began his rise as the leader of a small nomad band. By guile and force of arms, he established dominion over the lands between the Oxus and Jaxartes rivers (Transoxania) by the 1360s. He then, for three decades, led his mounted archers to subdue each state from Mongolia to the Mediterranean. He was the last of the mighty conquerors of Central Asia to achieve such military successes as leader of the nomad warrior lords, ruling both agricultural and pastoral peoples on an imperial scale. The poverty, bloodshed, and desolation caused by his campaigns gave rise to many legends, which in turn inspired such works as Christopher Marlowe's *Tamburlaine the Great*.

The name Timur Lenk (Turkish: "Timur the Lame"), as Timur was known, was a title of contempt used by his Persian enemies, which became Tamburlaine, or Tamerlane, in Europe. Timur was heir to a political, economic, and cultural heritage rooted in the pastoral peoples and nomad traditions of Central Asia. He and his compatriots cultivated the military arts and discipline of Genghis Khan and, as mounted archers and swordsmen, scorned the settled peasants. Timur never took up a permanent abode. He personally led his almost constantly campaigning forces, enduring extremes of desert heat and lacerating cold. When not campaigning he moved with his army according to season and grazing facilities. His court traveled with him, including his household of one or more of his nine wives and concubines. He strove to make his capital, Samarkand, the most splendid city in Asia, but when he visited it he stayed only a few days and then moved back to the pavilions of his encampment in the plains beyond the city.

Timur was, above all, master of the military techniques developed by Genghis Khan, using every weapon in the military and diplomatic armory of the day. He never missed an opportunity to exploit the weakness (political, economic, or military) of the adversary or to use intrigue, treachery, and alliance to serve his purposes. The seeds of victory were sown among the ranks of the enemy by his agents before an engagement. He conducted sophisticated negotiations with both neighbouring and distant powers, which are recorded in diplomatic archives from England to China. In battle, the nomadic tactics of mobility and surprise were his major weapons of attack.

Timur's most lasting memorials are the Timurid architectural monuments of Samarkand, covered in azure, turquoise, gold, and alabaster mosaics; these are dominated by the great cathedral mosque, ruined by an earthquake but still soaring to an immense fragment of dome. His mausoleum, the Gur-e Amir, is one of the gems of Islamic art. Within the sepulchre he lies under a huge, broken slab of jade. The tomb was opened in 1941, having remained intact for half a millennium. The Soviet Archaeological Commission found the skeleton of a man who, though lame in both right limbs, must have been of powerful physique and above-average height.

Timur's sons and grandsons fought over the succession when the Chinese expedition disbanded, but his dynasty survived in Central Asia for a century in spite of fratricidal strife. Samarkand became a centre of scholarship and science. It was here that Ulugh Beg, his grandson, set up an observatory and drew up the astronomical

Bronze statue in Tashkent, Uzbekistan, showing Timur on his horse. Tim Graham/Getty Images

tables that were later used by the English royal astronomer in the 17th century. During the Timurid renaissance of the 15th century, Herat, southeast of Samarkand, became the home of the brilliant school of Persian miniaturists. At the beginning of the 16th century, when the dynasty ended in Central Asia, his descendant Babur established himself in Kabul and then conquered Delhi, to found the Muslim line of Indian emperors known as the Great Mughals.

ARABS

When the Fatimids conquered Egypt in 969, they left a governor named Ziri in the Maghrib. In the 1040s the dynasty founded by Ziri declared its independence from the Fatimids, but it too was challenged by breakaways such as the Zanatah in Morocco and the Hammadids in Algeria. Gradually the Zirids were restricted to the eastern Maghrib. There they were invaded from Egypt by two Bedouin Arab tribes, the Banu Halil and the Banu Sulaym, at the instigation (1052) of the Fatimid ruler in Cairo. This mass migration of warriors as well as wives and children is known as the Hilalian invasion. Though initially disruptive, the Hilalian invasion had an important cultural impact: it resulted in a much greater spread of the Arabic language than had occurred in the 7th century and inaugurated the real Arabization of the Maghrib.

IMAZIGHEN

When the Arab conquerors arrived in the Maghrib in the 7th century, the indigenous peoples they met were the Imazighen (Berbers; singular Amazigh), a group of predominantly but not entirely migratory tribes who spoke a recognizably common Afro-Asiatic language with significant dialectal variations. Amazigh tribes could be found from present-day Morocco to present-day Algeria and from the Mediterranean to the Sahara. As among the Arabs, small tribal groupings of Imazighen occasionally formed short-lived confederations or became involved in caravan trade. No previous conqueror had tried to assimilate the Imazighen, but the Arabs quickly converted them and enlisted their aid in further conquests. Without their help, for example, Andalusia could never have been incorporated into the Islamicate state. At first only Imazighen nearer the coast were involved, but by the 11th century Muslim affiliation had begun to spread far into the Sahara.

THE SANHAJAH CONFEDERATION

One particular western Saharan Amazigh confederation, the Sanhajah, was responsible for the first Amazigh-directed effort to control the Maghrib. The Sanhajah were camel herders who traded mined salt for gold with the black kingdoms of the south. By the 11th century their power in the western Sahara was being threatened by expansion both from other Amazigh tribes, centred at Sijilmassa, and from the Soninke state at Ghana to the south, which had actually captured their capital of Audaghost in 990. The subsequent revival of their fortunes parallels Muhammad's revitalization of the Arabs 500 years earlier, in that Muslim ideology reinforced their efforts to unify several smaller groups. The Sanhajah had been in contact with Islam since the 9th century, but their distance from major centres of Muslim life had kept their knowledge of the faith minimal. In 1035, however, Yahya ibn Ibrahim, a chief from one of their tribes, the Gudalah, went on *hajj*. For the Maghribi pilgrim, the cultural impact of the *hajj* was experienced not only in Mecca and Medina but also on the many stops along the 3,000-mile (4,828 km) overland route. When Yahya returned, he was accompanied by a teacher from Nafis (in present-day Libya), 'Abd Allah ibn Yasin, who would instruct the Imazighen in Islam as teachers under 'Umar I had instructed the Arab fighters in the first Muslim garrisons. Having met with little initial success, the two are said to have retired to a *ribat*, a fortified place of seclusion, perhaps as far south as an island in the Sénégal River, to pursue a purer religious life. The followers they attracted to that *ribat* were known, by derivation, as *al-murabitun* (Arabic: "those who are garrisoned"). The dynasty they founded came to be known by the same name, or Almoravids in its Anglicized form. In 1042 Ibn Yasin declared a jihad against the Sanhajah tribes, including his own, as people who had embraced Islam but then failed to practice it properly. By his death in 1059, the Sanhajah confederation had been restored under an Islamic ideology, and the conquest of Morocco, which lacked strong leadership, was under way.

THE ALMORAVID DYNASTY

A consultative body of *ulama* took over Ibn Yasin's spiritual role. His successor as military commander was Abu Bakr ibn 'Umar. While pursuing the campaign against Morocco, Abu Bakr had to go south, leaving his cousin Yusuf ibn Tashufin as his deputy. When Abu Bakr tried to return, Ibn Tashufin turned him back to the south, where he remained until his death in 1087. Under Ibn Tashufin's leadership, by 1082, Almoravid control extended as far as Algiers. In 1086 Ibn Tashufin responded to a request for help from the Andalusian party kings, unable to defend themselves against the Christian kingdoms in the north, such as Castile. By 1110 all Muslim states in Andalusia had come under Almoravid control.

Like most other Jama'i-Sunni rulers of his time, Ibn Tashufin had himself "appointed" deputy by the caliph in Baghdad. He also based his authority on the claim to bring correct Islam to peoples who had strayed from it. For him, "correct" Islam meant the Shari'ah as developed by the Maliki *faqih*s, who played a key role in the Almoravid state by working out the application of the Shari'ah to everyday problems. Like their contemporaries elsewhere, they received stipends from the government, sat in the ruler's council, went on campaign with him, and gave him recommendations (fatwas) on important decisions. This was an approach to Islam far more current than the one it had replaced but still out of touch with the liveliest intellectual developments. During the next phase of Amazigh activism, newer trends from the east reached the Maghrib.

A second major Amazigh movement originated in a revolt begun against Almoravid rule in 1125 by Ibn Tumart, a settled Masmudah Amazigh from the Atlas Mountains. Like Ibn Yasin, Ibn Tumart had been inspired by the *hajj*, which he used as an opportunity to study in Baghdad, Cairo, and Jerusalem, acquainting himself with all current schools of Islamic thought and becoming a disciple of the ideas of the recently deceased al-Ghazali. Emulating his social activism, Ibn Tumart was inspired to act on the familiar Muslim dictum, "Command the good and forbid the reprehensible." His early attempts took two forms, disputations with the scholars of the Almoravid court and public chastisement of Muslims who in his view contradicted the rules of Islam. He went so far as to throw the

Almoravid ruler's sister off her horse because she was unveiled in public. His activities aroused hostility, and he fled to the safety of his own people. There, like Muhammad, he grew from teacher of a personal following to leader of a social movement.

Like many subsequent reformers, especially in Africa and other outlying Muslim lands, Ibn Tumart used Muhammad's career as a model. He interpreted the Prophet's rejection and retreat as an emigration (*hijrah*) that enabled him to build a community, and he divided his followers into *muhajirun* ("fellow emigrants") and *ansar* ("helpers"). He preached the idea of surrender to God to a people who had strayed from it. Thus could Muhammad's ability to bring about radical change through renewal be invoked without actually claiming the prophethood that he had sealed forever. Ibn Tumart further based his legitimacy on his claim to be a sharif (descendant of Muhammad) and the *mahdi*, not in the Shi'ite sense but in the more general sense of a human sent to restore pure faith. In his view Almoravid students of legal knowledge were so concerned with pursuing the technicalities of the law that they had lost the purifying fervour of their own founder, Ibn Yasin. They even failed to maintain proper Muslim behaviour, be it the veiling of women in public or the condemning of the use of wine, musical instruments, and other unacceptable, if not strictly illegal, forms of pleasure. Like many Muslim revitalizers before and since, Ibn Tumart decried the way in which the law had taken on a life of its own, and he called upon Muslims to rely on the original and only reliable sources, the Qur'an and Hadith. Although he opposed irresponsible rationalism in the law, in matters of theological discourse he leaned toward the limited rationalism of the Ash'arite school, which was becoming so popular in the eastern Muslim lands. Like the Ash'arites, he viewed the unity of God as one of Islam's fundamentals and denounced any reading of the Qur'an that led to anthropomorphism. Because he focused on attesting the unity of God (*tawhid*), he called his followers al-Muwahhidun (Almohads), "Those Who Attest the Unity of God." Ibn Tumart's movement signifies the degree to which Maghribis could participate in the intellectual life of Islamdom as a whole, but his need to use the Tamazight language for his many followers who did not know Arabic also illustrates the limits of interregional discourse.

THE ALMOHAD DYNASTY

By 1147, 17 years after Ibn Tumart's death, Almohads had replaced Almoravids in all their Maghribi and Andalusian territories. In Andalusia their arrival slowed the progress of the Christian Reconquista. There, as in the Maghrib, arts and letters were encouraged. An example is an important movement of *falsafah* that included Ibn Tufayl, Ibn al-'Arabi, and Ibn Rushd (Latin Averroës), the Andalusian *qadi* and physician whose interpretations of Aristotle became so important for medieval European Christianity. During the late Almohad period in Andalusia the intercommunal nature of Islamicate civilization became especially noticeable in the work of non-Muslim thinkers, such as Moses Maimonides, who participated in trends outside their own communities even at the expense of criticism from within. By the early 13th century, Almohad power began to decline; a defeat in 1212 at Las Navas de Tolosa by the Christian kings of the north forced a retreat to the Maghrib. But the impact of Almohad cultural patronage on Andalusia long outlasted Almohad political power. Successor dynasties in surviving Muslim states were responsible for some of the highest cultural achievements of Andalusian Muslims, among them the Alhambra palace in Granada. Furthermore, the 400-year southward movement of the Christian-Muslim frontier resulted, ironically, in some of the most intense Christian-Muslim interaction in Andalusian history. The Cid could fight for both sides; Muslims, as Mudejars, could live under Christian rule and contribute to its culture; Jews could translate Arabic and Hebrew texts into Castilian. Almohads were replaced in the Maghrib as well, through a revolt by their own governors—the Hafsids in Tunis and the Marinid Amazigh dynasty in Fès. There too, however, Almohad influence outlasted their political presence: both towns became centres, in distinctively Maghribi form, of Islamicate culture and Islamic piety.

CONTINUED SPREAD OF ISLAMIC INFLUENCE

As the Maghrib became firmly and distinctively Muslim, Islam moved south. The spread of Muslim identity into the Sahara and the involvement of Muslim peoples, especially the Tuareg, in trans-Saharan trade provided several natural channels of influence. By the time of the Marinids, Hafsids, and Mamluks, several major trade routes had established crisscrossing lines of communication: from Cairo to Timbuktu, from Tripoli to Bornu and Lake Chad, from Tunis to Timbuktu at the bend of the Niger River, and from Fès and Tafilalt through major Saharan entrepôts into Ghana and Mali. The rise at Timbuktu of Mali, the first great western Sudanic empire with a Muslim ruler, attested the growing incorporation of sub-Saharan Africa into the North African orbit. The reign of Mansa Musa, who even went on pilgrimage, demonstrated the influence of Islam on at least the upper echelons of African society.

The best picture of Islamdom in the 14th century appears in the work of a remarkable Maghribi *qadi* and traveler, Ibn Battutah (1304–1368/69 or 1377). In 1325, the year that Mansa Musa went on pilgrimage, Ibn Battutah also left for Mecca, from his hometown of Tangiers. He was away for almost 30 years, visiting most of Islamdom, including Andalusia, all of the Maghrib, Mali, Syria, Arabia, Iran, India, the Maldive Islands, and, he claimed, China. He described the unity within diversity that was one of Islamdom's most prominent features. Although local customs often seemed at variance with his notion of pure Islamic practice, he felt at home everywhere. Despite the divisions that had occurred during Islam's 700-year history, a Muslim could attend the Friday worship session in any Muslim town in the world and feel comfortable, a claim that is difficult if not impossible to make for any other major religious tradition at any time in its history. By the time of Ibn Battutah's death, Islamdom comprised the most far-flung yet interconnected set of societies in the world. As one author has pointed out, Thomas Aquinas (*c.* 1224–74) might have been read from Spain to Hungary and from Sicily to Norway, but Ibn al-'Arabi (1165–1240) was read from Spain to Sumatra and from the Swahili coast to Kazan on the Volga River. By the end of the period of migration and renewal, Islam had begun to spread not only into sub-Saharan Africa but also into the southern seas with the establishment of a Muslim presence in the Straits of Malacca. Conversion to Islam across its newer frontiers was at first limited to a small elite, who supplemented local religious practices with Muslim ones. Islam could offer not only a unifying religious system but also social techniques, including alphabetic literacy, a legal system applicable to daily life, a set of administrative institutions, and a body of science and technology—all capable of enhancing the power of ruling elements and of tying them into a vast and lucrative trading network.

The period of migration and renewal exposed both the potentiality and the limitations of government by tribal peoples. This great problem of Islamicate history received its most sophisticated analysis from a Maghribi Muslim named Ibn Khaldun (1332–1406), a contemporary of Petrarch. His family had migrated from Andalusia to the Maghrib, and he himself was born in Hafsid territory. He was both a *faylasuf* and a *qadi*, a combination more common in Andalusia and the Maghrib than anywhere else in Islamdom. His *falsafah* was activist; he strove to use his political wisdom to the benefit of one of the actual rulers of the day. To this end he moved from one court to another before becoming disillusioned and retiring to Mamluk Cairo as a *qadi*. His life thus demonstrated the importance and the constraints of royal patronage as a stimulant to intellectual creativity. In his *Muqaddimah* (the introduction to his multivolume world history) he used his training in *falsafah* to discern patterns in history. Transcending the critiques of historical method made by historians of the Buyid period, such as al-Mas'udi, Ibn Miskawayh, and al-Suli, Ibn Khaldun established careful standards of evidence. Whereas Muslim historians conventionally subscribed to the view that God passed sovereignty and hegemony (*dawlah*) from one dynasty to another through his divine wisdom, Ibn Khaldun explained it in terms of a cycle of natural and inevitable stages. By his day it had become apparent that tribally organized migratory peoples, so favoured by much of the ecology of the Maghrib and the Nile-to-Oxus region, could easily acquire military superiority over settled peoples if they could capitalize on the inherently stronger group feeling (*asabiyyah*) that kinship provides. Once in power, according to Ibn Khaldun, conquering groups pass through a phase in which a small number of "builders" among them bring renewed vitality to their conquered lands. As the family disperses itself among sedentary peoples and ceases to live the hard life of migration, it becomes soft from the prosperity it has brought and begins to degenerate. Then internal rivalries and jealousies force one member of the family to become a king who must rely on mercenary troops and undermine his own prosperity by paying for them. In the end, the ruling dynasty falls prey to a new tribal group with fresh group feeling. Thus did Ibn Khaldun call attention to the unavoidable instability of all premodern Muslim dynasties, caused by their lack of the regularized patterns of succession that were beginning to develop in European dynasties.

CHAPTER 6

CONSOLIDATION AND EXPANSION (1405–1683)

After the death of Timur in 1405, power began to shift from migrating peoples to sedentary populations living in large centralized empires. After about 1683, when the last Ottoman campaign against Vienna failed, the great empires for which this period is so famous began to shrink and weaken, just as western Europeans first began to show their potential for worldwide expansion and domination. When the period began, Muslim lands had begun to recover from the devastating effects of the Black Death (1346–48), and many were prospering. Muslims had the best opportunity in history to unite the settled world, but by the end of the period they had been replaced by Europeans as the leading contenders for this role. Muslims were now forced into direct and repeated contact with Europeans, through armed hostilities as well as through commercial interactions, and often the Europeans competed well. Yet Muslim power was so extensive and the western Europeans such an unexpected source of competition that Muslims were able to realize that their situation had changed only after they no longer had the strength to resist. Furthermore, the existence of several strong com-petitive Muslim states militated against a united response to the Europeans and could even encourage some Muslims to align themselves with the European enemies of others.

In this period, long after Islamdom was once thought to have peaked, centralized absolutism reached its height, aided in part by the exploitation of gunpowder warfare and in part by new ways to fuse spiritual and military authority. Never before had Islamicate ideals and institu-tions better demonstrated their ability to encourage political centralization or to support a Muslim style of life where there was no organized state, be it in areas where Islam had been long established or in areas where it was newly arrived. The major states of this period impressed contemporary Europeans; in them some of the greatest Islamicate artistic achievements were made. In this period Muslims formed the cultural patterns that they brought into modern times, and adherence to Islam expanded to approximately its current distribution. As adherence to Islam expanded, far-flung cultural regions began to take on a life of their own. The unity of several of these regions was expressed through empire—the Ottomans in south-eastern Europe, Anatolia, the eastern Maghrib, Egypt, and Syria; the Safavids in Iran and Iraq; the Indo-Timurids (Mughals) in India. In these empires, Sunni and Shi'ite became identities on a much larger scale than ever before, expressing competition between large populations. Simultaneously Shi'ism acquired a permanent base from which to generate international opposition. Elsewhere, less formal and often commercial ties bound Muslims from distant locales. Growing commercial and political links between Morocco and the western Sudan pro-duced a trans-Saharan Maghribi Islam. Egyptian Islam influenced the central and eastern Sudan. And steady con-tacts between East Africa, South Arabia, southern Iran, southwest India, and the southern seas promoted a recognizable Indian Ocean Islam, with Persian as its lingua franca. In fact, Persian became the closest yet to an international language; but the expansion and naturalization of Islam also fostered a number of local languages into vehicles for Islamicate administration and high culture—Ottoman, Chagatai, Swahili, Urdu, and Malay. Everywhere Muslims were confronting adherents of other religions, and new converts often practiced Islam without abandoning their previous practices. The various ways in which Muslims responded to religious syncretism and plurality continue to be elaborated to the present day.

This was a period of major realignments and expansion. The extent of Muslim presence in the Eastern Hemisphere in the early 15th century was easily discernible, but only with difficulty could one have imagined that it could soon produce three of the greatest empires in world history. From the Atlantic to the Pacific, from the Balkans to Sumatra, Muslim rulers presided over relatively small kingdoms; but nowhere could the emergence of a world-class dynasty be predicted. In Andalusia only one Muslim state, Granada, remained to resist Christian domination of the Iberian Peninsula. The Maghrib, isolated between an almost all-Christian Iberia and an eastward-looking Mamluk Egypt and Syria, was divided between the Marinids and Hafsids. Where the Sahara shades off into the Sudanic belt, the empire of Mali at Gao was ruled by a Muslim and included several Saharan "port" cities, such as Timbuktu, that were centres of Muslim learning. On the Swahili coast, oriented as always more toward the Indian Ocean than toward its own hinterland, several small Muslim polities centred on key ports such as Kilwa. In western Anatolia and the Balkan Peninsula the Ottoman state under Sultan Mehmed I was recovering from its defeat by Timur. Iraq and western Iran were the domains of Turkic tribal dynasties known as the Black Sheep (Kara Koyunlu) and the White Sheep (Ak Koyunlu). They shared a border in Iran with myriad princelings of the Timurid line and the neo-Mongol, neo-Timurid Uzbek state ruled in Transoxania. North of the Caspian Sea, several Muslim khanates ruled as far north as Moscow and Kazan. In India, even though Muslims constituted a minority, they were beginning to assert their power everywhere except the south, which was ruled by Vijayanagar. In Islamdom's far southeast, the Muslim state of Samudra held sway in Sumatra, and the rulers of the Moluccas had recently converted to Islam and begun to expand into the southern Malay Peninsula. Even where no organized state existed, as in the outer reaches of Central Asia and into southern China, scattered small Muslim communities persisted, often centred on oases. By the end of this period, Islamdom's borders had retreated only in Russia and Iberia, but these losses were more than compensated by continuing expansion in Europe, Africa, Central Asia, and South and Southeast Asia. Almost everywhere this plethora of states had undergone realignment and consolidation, based on experimentation with forms of legitimation and structure.

OTTOMANS

CONTINUATION OF OTTOMAN RULE

After the Ottoman state's devastating defeat by Timur, its leaders had to retain the vitality of the warrior spirit (without its unruliness and intolerance) and the validation of the Shari'ah (without its confining independence). In 1453 Mehmed II (the Conqueror) fulfilled the warrior ideal by conquering Constantinople (soon to be known as Istanbul), putting an end to the Byzantine Empire, and subjugating the local Christian and Jewish populations. Even by then, however, a new form of legitimation was taking shape. The Ottomans continued to wage war against Christians on the frontier and to levy and convert (through the *devsirme*) young male Christians to serve in the sultan's household and army, but warriors were being pensioned off with land grants and replaced by troops more beholden to the sultan. Except for those forcibly converted, the rest of the non-Muslim population was protected for payment according to the Shari'ah and the preference of the *ulema* (the Turkish spelling of *ulama*), and organized into self-governing communities known as *millets*. Furthermore, the sultans began to claim the caliphate because they met two of its traditional qualifications: they ruled justly, in principle according to the Shari'ah, and they defended and extended the frontiers, as in their conquest of Mamluk Egypt, Syria, and the holy cities in 1516–17. Meanwhile, they began to undercut the traditional oppositional stance of the *ulema* by building on Seljuq and Mongol practice in three ways: they promoted state-supported training of *ulema*; they defined and paid holders of religious offices as part of the military; and they aggressively asserted the validity of dynastic law alongside Shari'ah. Simultaneously, they emphasized their inheritance of Byzantine legitimacy by transforming Byzantine symbols, such as Hagia Sophia (Church of the Divine Wisdom), into symbols for Islam, and by favouring their empire's European part, called, significantly, Rum.

REIGN OF SÜLEYMAN I

The classical Ottoman system crystallized during the reign of Süleyman I (the Lawgiver; ruled 1520–66). He also pushed the empire's borders almost to their farthest limits—to the walls of Vienna in the northwest, throughout the Maghrib up to Morocco in the southwest, into

SÜLEYMAN I

The only son of Sultan Selim I, Süleyman I (1494/95–1566) succeeded his father in September 1520 and began his reign with campaigns against the Christian powers in central Europe and the Mediterranean. Belgrade fell to him in 1521 and Rhodes, long under the rule of the Knights of St. John, in 1522. At Mohács, in August 1526, Süleyman broke the military strength of Hungary, the Hungarian king, Louis II, losing his life in the battle.

The vacant throne of Hungary was now claimed by Ferdinand I, the Habsburg archduke of Austria, and by John (János Zápolya), who was *voivode* (lord) of Transylvania, and the candidates of the "native" party opposed to the prospect of Habsburg rule. Süleyman agreed to recognize John as a vassal king of Hungary, and in 1529, hoping to remove at one blow all further intervention by the Habsburgs, he laid siege to Vienna. Difficulties of time and distance and of bad weather and lack of supplies, no less than the resistance of the Christians, forced the sultan to raise the siege.

The campaign was successful, however, in a more immediate sense, for John was to rule thereafter over most of Hungary until his death, in 1540. A second great campaign in 1532, notable for the brilliant Christian defense of Güns, ended as a mere foray into Austrian border territories. The sultan, preoccupied with affairs in the East and convinced that Austria was not to be overcome at one stroke, granted a truce to the archduke Ferdinand in 1533.

The death of John in 1540 and the prompt advance of Austrian forces once more into central Hungary drove Süleyman to modify profoundly the solution that he had imposed in the time of John. His campaigns of 1541 and 1543 led to the emergence of three distinct Hungarys—Habsburg Hungary in the extreme north and west; Ottoman Hungary along the middle Danube, a region under direct and permanent military occupation by the Ottomans and with its main centre at Buda; and Transylvania, a vassal state dependent on the Porte and in the hands of John Sigismund, the son of John Zápolya.

Between 1543 and 1562 the war in Hungary continued, broken by truces and with few notable changes on either side; the most important was the Ottoman capture of the Banat of Temesvár (Timisoara) in 1532. After long negotiations a peace recognizing the status quo in Hungary was signed in 1562.

During the course of his rule, Süleyman waged three major campaigns against Persia. The first (1534–35) gave the Ottomans control over the region of Erzurum in eastern Asia Minor and also witnessed the Ottoman conquest of Iraq, a success that rounded off the achievements of Selim I. The second campaign (1548–49) brought much of the area around Lake Van under Ottoman rule, but the third (1554–55) served rather as a warning to the Ottomans of the difficulty of subduing the Safavid state in Persia. The first formal peace between the Ottomans and the Safavids was signed in 1555, but it offered no clear solution to the problems confronting the Ottoman sultan on his eastern frontier.

The naval strength of the Ottomans became formidable in the reign of Süleyman. Khayr al-Din, known in the West as Barbarossa, became *kapudan* (admiral) of the Ottoman fleet and won a sea fight off Preveza, Greece (1538), against the combined fleets of Venice and Spain, which gave to the Ottomans the naval initiative in the Mediterranean until the Battle of Lepanto in 1571. Tripoli in North Africa fell to the Ottomans in 1551. A strong Spanish expedition against Tripoli was crushed at Jarbah (Djerba) in 1560, but the Ottomans failed to capture Malta from the Knights of St. John in 1565. Ottoman naval power was felt at this time even as far afield as India, where a fleet sent out from Egypt made an unsuccessful attempt in 1538 to take the town of Diu from the Portuguese.

Süleyman's later years were troubled by conflict between his sons. Mustafa had become by 1553 a focus of disaffection in Asia Minor and was executed in that year on the order of the sultan. There followed during 1559–61 a conflict between the princes Selim and Bayezid over the succession to the throne, which ended with the defeat and execution of Bayezid. Süleyman himself died while besieging the fortress of Szigetvár in Hungary.

Iraq to the east, and to the Yemen in the southeast. During Süleyman's reign the Ottomans even sent an expedition into the southern seas to help Aceh against the Portuguese colonizers. In theory, Süleyman presided over a balanced four-part structure: the palace household, which contained all of the sultan's wives, concubines, children, and servants; the bureaucracy (chancery and treasury); the armed forces; and the religious establishment. Important positions in the army and bureaucracy went to the cream of the *devsirme*, Christian youths converted to Islam and put through special training at the capital to be the sultan's personal "slaves." *Ulema* who acquired government posts had undergone systematic training at the major *medrese*s (madrasahs) and so in the Ottoman state were more integrated than were their counterparts in other states. Yet they were freeborn Muslims, not brought into the system as slaves of the sultan. The ruling class communicated in a language developed for their use only, Ottoman, which combined Turkic syntax with largely Arabic and Persian vocabulary. It was in this new language that so many important figures demonstrated the range and sophistication of Ottoman interests, such as the historian Mustafa Naima, the encyclopaedist Kâtip Çelebi, and the traveler Evliya Çelebi. The splendour of the Ottoman capital owed not a little to Süleyman's chief architect, the Greek *devsirme* recruit Sinan, who transformed the city's skyline with magnificent mosques and *medrese*s.

THE EXTENT OF OTTOMAN ADMINISTRATION

Even in North Africa and the Fertile Crescent, where Ottoman rule was indirect, the effect of its administration, especially its land surveys and *millet* and tax systems, could be felt. Remnants of the Ottoman system continue to play a role in the political life of modern states such as Israel and Lebanon, despite the fact that Ottoman control had already begun to relax by the first quarter of the 17th century. By then control of the state treasury was passing, through land grants, into the hands of local *a'yan*, and they

Ink and gold leaf representation of the long-ruling sultan of the Ottoman Empire, Süleyman I, as a young man. Nakkas Osman/The Bridgeman Art Library/Getty Images

gradually became the real rulers, serving local rather than imperial interests. Meanwhile discontinuance of the *devsirme* and the rise of hereditary succession to imperial offices shut off new sources of vitality. Monarchs, confined to the palace during their youth, became weaker and participated less in military affairs and government councils. As early as 1630, Sultan Murad IV was presented by one of his advisers with a memorandum explaining the causes of the perceived decline and urging a restoration of the system as it had existed under Süleyman. Murad IV tried to restore Ottoman efficiency and central control, and his efforts were continued by subsequent sultans aided by a talented family of ministers known as the Köprülüs. However, during a war with the Holy League (Austria, Russia, Venice, and Poland) from 1683 to 1699, in which a major attack on Vienna failed (1683), the Ottomans suffered their first serious losses to an enemy and exposed the weakness of their system to their European neighbours. They signed two treaties, at Carlowitz in 1699 and at Passarowitz in 1718, that confirmed their losses in southeastern Europe, signified their inferiority to the Habsburg coalition, and established the defensive posture they would maintain into the 20th century.

SAFAVIDS

The Safavid state began not from a band of *ghazi* warriors but from a local Sufi *tariqah* of Ardabil in the Azerbaijan region of Iran. The *tariqah* was named after its founder, Shaykh Safi al-Din (1252/53–1334), a local holy man. As for many *tariqah*s and other voluntary associations, Sunni and Shi'ite alike, affection for the family of 'Ali was a channel for popular support. During the 15th century Shaykh Safi's successors transformed their local *tariqah* into an interregional movement by translating 'Alid loyalism into full-fledged Imami Shi'ism. By asserting that they were the Sufi "perfect men" of their time as well as descendants and representatives of the last imam, they strengthened the support of their Turkic tribal disciples (known as the Kizilbash, or "Red Heads," because of their symbolic 12-fold red headgear). They also attracted support outside Iran, especially in eastern Anatolia (where the anti-Ottoman Imami Bektashi *tariqah* was strong), in Syria, the Caucasus, and Transoxania. The ability of the Iranian Shi'ite state to serve as a source of widespread local opposition outside of Iran was again to become dramatically apparent many years later, with the rise of the ayatollah Ruhollah Khomeini's Islamic republic in the late 1970s.

EXPANSION IN IRAN AND BEYOND

By 1501 the Safavids were able to defeat the Ak Koyunlu rulers of northern Iran, whereupon their teenage leader Isma'il I (ruled 1501–24) had himself proclaimed shah, using that pre-Islamic title for the first time in almost 900 years and thereby invoking the glory of ancient Iran. The Safavids thus asserted a multivalent legitimacy that flew in the face of Ottoman claims to have restored caliphal authority for all Muslims. Eventually, irritant became threat: by 1510, when Isma'il had conquered all of Iran (to approximately its present frontiers) as well as the Fertile Crescent, he began pushing against the Uzbeks in the east and the Ottomans in the west, both of whom already suffered from significant Shi'ite opposition that could easily be aroused by Safavid successes. Having to fight on two fronts was the most difficult military problem any Muslim empire could face. According to the persisting Mongol pattern, the army was a single force attached to the household of the ruler and moving with him at all times; so the size of an area under effective central control was limited to the farthest points that could be reached in a single campaign season. After dealing with his eastern front, Isma'il turned west. At Chaldiran (1514) in northwestern Iraq, having refused to use gunpowder weapons, Isma'il suffered the kind of defeat at Ottoman hands that the Ottomans had suffered from Timur. Yet through the war of words waged in a body of correspondence between Shah Isma'il and the Ottoman sultan Selim I, and through the many invasions from both fronts that occurred during the next 60 years, the Safavid state survived and prospered. Still living off its position at the crossroads of the trans-Asian trade that had supported all previous empires in Iraq and Iran, it was not yet undermined by the gradual emergence of more significant sea routes to the south.

The first requirement for the survival of the Safavid state was the conversion of its predominantly Jama'i-Sunni population to Imami Shi'ism. This was accomplished by a government-run effort supervised by the state-appointed leader of the religious community, the *sadr*. Gradually forms of piety emerged that were specific to Safavid Shi'ism; they centred on pilgrimage to key sites connected with the imams, as well as on the annual remembering and reenacting of the key event in Shi'ite history, the caliph Yazid I's destruction of Imam al-Husayn at Karbala' on the 10th of Muharram, AH 61 (680 CE). The 10th of Muharram, or 'Ashura', already marked throughout Islamdom with fasting, became for Iranian Shi'ites the centre of the religious calendar. The first 10 days of Muharram became a period of communal mourning, during which the pious imposed suffering on themselves to identify with their martyrs of old, listened to sermons, and recited appropriate elegiac poetry. In later Safavid times the name for this mourning, *ta'ziyeh*, also came to be applied to passion plays performed to reenact events surrounding al-Husayn's martyrdom. Through the depths of their empathetic suffering, Shi'ites could help to overturn the injustice of al-Husayn's martyrdom at the end of time, when all wrongs would be righted, all wrongdoers punished, and all true followers of the imams rewarded.

SHAH 'ABBAS I

The state also survived because Isma'il's successors moved, like the Ottomans, toward a type of legitimation different from the one that had brought them to power. This development began in the reign of Tahmasp (1524–76) and culminated in the reign of the greatest Safavid shah, 'Abbas I (ruled 1588–1629). Since Isma'il's time, the tribes had begun to lose faith in the Safavid monarch as spiritual leader. Now 'Abbas appealed for support more as absolute monarch and less as the charismatic Sufi master or incarnated imam. At the same time, he freed himself from his unruly tribal emirs by depending more and more on a paid army of converted Circassian, Georgian, and Armenian Christian captives. Meanwhile, he continued to rely on a large bureaucracy headed by a chief minister with limited responsibilities, but, unlike his Ottoman contemporaries, he distanced members of the religious community from state involvement while allowing them an independent source of support in their administration of the *waqf* system. Because the Shi'ite *ulama* had a tradition of independence that made them resist incorporation into the military "household" of the shah, 'Abbas's policies were probably not unpopular, but they eventually undermined his state's legitimacy. By the end of the period under discussion, it was the religious leaders, the *mujtahid*s, who would claim to be the spokesmen for the hidden imam. Having shared the ideals of the military patronage state, the Ottoman state became more firmly militarized and religious, as the Safavid became more civilianized and secular.

The long-term consequences of this breach between government and the religious institution were extensive, culminating in the establishment of the Islamic republic of Iran in 1978.

'Abbas expressed his new role by moving his capital about 1597–98 to Esfahan in Fars, the central province of the ancient pre-Islamic Iranian empires and symbolically more Persian than Turkic. Esfahan, favoured by a high and scenic setting, became one of the most beautiful cities in the world, leading its boosters to say that "Esfahan is half the world." It came to contain, often thanks to royal patronage, myriad palaces, gardens, parks, mosques, *medrese*s, caravansaries, workshops, and public baths. Many of these still stand, including the famed Masjed-e Shah, a mosque that shares the great central mall with an enormous covered bazaar and many other structures. It was there that 'Abbas received diplomatic and commercial visits from Europeans, including a Carmelite mission from Pope Clement XIII (1604) and the adventuring Sherley brothers from Elizabethan England. Just as his visitors hoped to use him to their own advantage, 'Abbas hoped to use them to his, as sources of firearms and military technology, or as pawns in his economic warfare against the Ottomans, in which he was willing to seek help from apparently anyone, including the Russians, Portuguese, and Habsburgs.

Under Safavid rule, Iran in the 16th and 17th centuries became the centre of a major cultural flowering expressed through the Persian language and through the visual arts. This flowering extended to Safavid neighbour states as well—Ottomans, Uzbeks, and Indo-Timurids. Like other Shi'ite dynasties before them, the Safavids encouraged the development of *falsafah* as a companion to Shi'ite esotericism and cosmology. Two major thinkers, Mir Damad and his disciple Mulla Sadra, members of the Ishraqi, or illuminationist, school, explored the realm of images or symbolic imagination as a way to understand issues of human meaningfulness. The Safavid period was also important for the development of Shi'ite Shari'ah-minded studies, and it produced a major historian, Iskandar Beg Munshi, chronicler of 'Abbas's reign.

DECLINE OF CENTRAL AUTHORITY

None of 'Abbas's successors was his equal, though his state, ever weaker, survived for a century. The last effective shah, Husayn I (1694–1722), could defend himself neither from tribal raiding in the capital nor from interfering *mujtahid*s led by Muhammad Baqir Majlisi (whose writings later would be important in the Islamic republic of Iran). In 1722, when Mahmud of Qandahar led an Afghan tribal raid into Iran from the east, he easily took Esfahan and destroyed what was left of central authority.

INDO-TIMURIDS (MUGHALS)

FOUNDATION BY BABUR

Although the Mongol-Timurid legacy influenced the Ottoman and Safavid states, it had its most direct impact on Babur (1483–1530), the adventurer's adventurer and founder of the third major empire of the period. Babur's father, 'Umar Shaykh Mirza (died 1494) of Fergana, was one among many Timurid "princes" who continued to rule small pieces of the lands their great ancestor had conquered. After his father's death the 11-year-old Babur, who claimed descent not only from Timur but also from Genghis Khan (on his mother's side), quickly faced one of the harshest realities of his time and place—too many princes for too few kingdoms. In his youth he dreamed of capturing Samarkand as a base for reconstructing Timur's empire. For a year after the Safavid defeat of the Uzbek Muhammad Shaybani Khan, Babur and his Chagatai followers did hold Samarkand, as Safavid vassals. But, when the Safavids were in turn defeated, Babur lost not only Samarkand but his native Fergana as well. He was forced to retreat to Kabul, which he had occupied in 1504. From there he never restored Timur's empire. Rather, barred from moving north or west, he took the Timurid legacy south, to a land on which Timur had made only the slightest impression.

When Babur turned toward northern India, it was ruled from Delhi by the Lodi sultans, one of many local Turkic dynasties scattered through the subcontinent. In 1526 at Panipat, Babur met and defeated the much larger Lodi army. In his victory he was aided, like the Ottomans at Chaldiran, by his artillery. By his death just four years later, he had laid the foundation for a remarkable empire, known most commonly as the Mughal (i.e., Mongol) Empire. It is more properly called Indo-Timurid because the Chagatai Turks were distinct from the surviving Mongols of the time

This 16th-century work by an Indian artist shows Mughal emperor Babur with his son Humayan. Dip Chand/ The Bridgeman Art Library/ Getty Images

and because Babur and his successors acknowledge Timur as the founder of their power.

Babur is also remembered for his memoirs, the *Babur-nameh*. Written in Chagatai, then an emerging Islamicate literary language, his work gives a lively and compelling account of the wide range of interests, tastes, and sensibilities that made him so much a counterpart of his contemporary, the Italian Niccolò Machiavelli (1469–1527).

REIGN OF AKBAR

Süleyman's and 'Abbas's counterpart in the Indo-Timurid dynasty was their contemporary, Akbar (ruled 1556–1605), the grandson of Babur. At the time of his death, he ruled all of present-day India north of the Deccan plateau and Gondwana and more: one diagonal of his empire extended from the Hindu Kush to the Bay of Bengal; the other, from the Himalayas to the Arabian Sea. Like its contemporaries to the west, particularly the Ottomans, this state endured because of a regularized and equitable tax system that provided the central treasury with funds to support the ruler's extensive building projects as well as his *mansabdars*, the military and bureaucratic officers of the imperial service. For these key servants, Akbar, again like his counterparts to the west, relied largely on foreigners who were trained especially for his service. Like the Janissaries, the *mansabdars* were not supposed to inherit their offices, and, although they were assigned lands to supervise, they themselves were paid through the central treasury to assure their loyalty to the interests of the ruler.

Although Akbar's empire was, like Süleyman's and 'Abbas's, a variation on the theme of the military patronage state, his situation, and consequently many of his problems, differed from theirs in important ways. Islam was much more recently established in most of his empire than in either of the other two, and Muslims were not in the majority. Although the other two states were not religiously or ethnically homogeneous, the extent of their internal diversity could not compare with Akbar's, where Muslims and non-Muslims of every stripe alternately coexisted and came into conflict—Jacobites (members of the monophysite Syrian church), Sufis, Isma'ili Shi'ites, Zoroastrians, Jains, Jesuits, Jews, and Hindus. Consequently, Akbar was forced even more than the Ottomans to confront and address the issue of religious plurality. The option of aggressive conversion was virtually impossible in such a vast area, as was any version of the Ottoman *millet* system in a setting in which hundreds if not thousands of *millets* could be defined.

In some ways, Akbar faced in exaggerated form the situation that the Arab Muslims faced when they were a minority in the Nile-to-Oxus region in the 7th–9th centuries. Granting protected status to non-Muslims was legally and administratively justifiable, but, unless they could be kept from interacting too much with the Muslim population, Islam itself could be affected. The power of Sufi *tariqah*s like the influential Chishtis, and of the Hindu mystical movement of Guru Nanak, were already promoting intercommunal interaction and cross-fertilization. Akbar's response was different from that of the 'Abbasid caliph al-Mahdi. Instead of institutionalizing intolerance of non-Muslim influences and instead of hardening communal lines, Akbar banned intolerance and even the special tax on non-Muslims. To keep the *ulama* from objecting, he tried, for different reasons than had the Ottomans and Safavids, to tie them to the state financially. His personal curiosity about other religions was exemplary; with the help of Abu al-Fadl, his Sufi adviser and biographer, he established a kind of salon for religious discussion. A very small circle of personal disciples seems to have emulated

Akbar's own brand of *tawhid-i ilahi* ("divine oneness"). This appears to have been a general monotheism akin to what the *hanif*s of Mecca, and Muhammad himself, had once practiced, as well as to the boundary-breaking pantheistic awareness of great Sufis like Rumi and Ibn al-'Arabi, who was very popular in South and Southeast Asia. Akbar combined toleration for all religions with condemnation of practices that seemed to him humanly objectionable, such as enslavement and the immolation of widows.

CONTINUATION OF THE EMPIRE

For half a century, Akbar's first two successors, Jahangir and Shah Jahan, continued his policies. A rebuilt capital at Delhi was added to the old capitals of Fatehpur Sikri and Agra, site of Shah Jahan's most famous building, the Taj Mahal. The mingling of Hindu and Muslim traditions was expressed in all the arts, especially in naturalistic and sensuous painting; extremely refined and sophisticated design in ceramics, inlay work, and textiles; and in delicate yet monumental architecture. Shah Jahan's son, Dara Shikoh (1615–59), was a Sufi thinker and writer who tried to establish a common ground for Muslims and Hindus. In response to such attempts, a Shari'ah-minded movement of strict communalism arose, connected with a leader of the Naqshbandi *tariqah* named Shaykh Ahmad Sirhindi. With the accession of Aurangzeb (ruled 1658–1707), the tradition of ardent ecumenicism, which would reemerge several centuries later in a non-Muslim named Mohandas K. (Mahatma) Gandhi, was replaced with a stricter communalism that imposed penalties on protected non-Muslims and stressed the shah's role as leader of the Muslim community, by virtue of his enforcing the Shari'ah. Unlike the Ottoman and Safavid domains, the Indo-Timurid

The 17th-century Mughal-built Taj Mahal in Agra, India, is one of the most popular tourist attractions in the world. Tauseef Mustafa/AFP/Getty Images

empire was still expanding right up to the beginning of the 18th century, but the empire began to disintegrate shortly after the end of Aurangzeb's reign, when Safavid and Ottoman power were also declining rapidly.

SHAH JAHAN

Shah Jahan (1592–1666; known until 1628 as Prince Khurram) was the third son of the Mughal emperor Jahangir and the Rajput princess Manmati. In 1612 he married Arjumand Banu Begum, niece of Jahangir's wife Nur Jahan, and became one of the influential Nur Jahan clique of the middle period of Jahangir's reign. In 1622 Shah Jahan, ambitious to win the succession, rebelled, ineffectually roaming the empire until reconciled to Jahangir in 1625. After Jahangir's death in 1627, the support of Asaf Khan, Nur Jahan's brother, enabled Shah Jahan to proclaim himself emperor at Agra (February 1628).

Shah Jahan's reign was notable for successes against the Deccan states: by 1636 Ahmadnagar had been annexed and Golconda and Bijapur forced to become tributaries. Mughal power was also temporarily extended in the northwest. In 1638 the Persian governor of Kandahar, 'Ali Mardan Khan, surrendered that fortress to the Mughals. In 1646 Mughal forces occupied Badakhshan and Balkh, but in 1647 Balkh was relinquished, and attempts to reconquer it in 1649, 1652, and 1653 failed. The Persians reconquered Kandahar in 1649. Shah Jahan transferred his capital from Agra to Delhi in 1648, creating the new city of Shahjahanabad (now Old Delhi) there.

Shah Jahan had an almost insatiable passion for building. At his first capital, Agra, he undertook the building of two great mosques, the Pearl Mosque and the Great Mosque, as well as the superb mausoleum known as the Taj Mahal. The Taj Mahal is the masterpiece of his reign and was erected in memory of the favourite of his three queens, Mumtaz Mahal (the mother of Aurangzeb). At Delhi, Shah Jahan built a huge fortress-palace complex called the Red Fort as well as another Great Mosque, which is among the finest mosques in India. Shah Jahan's reign was also a period of great literary activity, and the arts of painting and calligraphy were not neglected. His court was one of great pomp and splendour, and his collection of jewels was probably the most magnificent in the world.

Indian writers have generally characterized Shah Jahan as the very ideal of a Muslim monarch. But though the splendour of the Mughal court reached its zenith under him, he also set in motion influences that finally led to the decline of the empire. His expeditions against Balkh and Badakhshan and his attempts to recover Kandahar brought the empire to the verge of bankruptcy. In religion, Shah Jahan was a more orthodox Muslim than Jahangir or his grandfather Akbar but a less orthodox one than Aurangzeb. He proved a relatively tolerant ruler toward his Hindu subjects.

In September 1657 Shah Jahan fell ill, precipitating a struggle for succession between his four sons, Dara Shikoh, Murad Bakhsh, Shah Shuja', and Aurangzeb. The victor, Aurangzeb, declared himself emperor in 1658 and strictly confined Shah Jahan in the fort at Agra until his death.

Between the 15th and the 18th century the use of coffee, tea, and tobacco, despite the objections of the *ulama*, became common in all three empires. Teahouses became important new centres for male socializing, in addition to the home, the mosque, the marketplace, and the public bath. (Female socializing was restricted largely to the home and the bath.) In the teahouses men could practice the already well-developed art of storytelling and take delight in the clever use of language. *The Thousand and One Nights* (*Alf laylah wa laylah*), the earliest extant manuscripts of which date from this period, and the stories of the Arabian hero 'Antar must have been popular, as were the tales of a wise fool known as Mullah Nasr al-Din in Persian (Nasreddin), Hoca in Turkish, and Juha in Arabic. The exploits of Nasr al-Din, sometimes in the guise of a Sufi dervish or royal adviser, often humorously portray centralized absolutism and mysticism:

Nasr al-Din was sent by the king to investigate the lore of various kinds of Eastern mystical teachers. They all recounted to him tales of the miracles and the sayings of the founders and great teachers, all long dead, of their schools. When he returned home, he submitted his report, which contained the single word "Carrots." He was called upon to explain himself. Nasr al-Din told the king: "The best part is buried; few know— except the farmer—by the green that there is orange underground; if you don't work for it, it will deteriorate; there are a great many donkeys associated with it."

TRANS-SAHARAN ISLAM

When the Ottomans expanded through the southern Mediterranean coast in the early 16th century, they were unable to incorporate Morocco, where a new state had been formed in reaction to the appearance of the Portuguese. The Portuguese were riding the momentum generated by their own seaborne expansion as well as by the fulfillment of the Reconquista and the establishment of an aggressively intolerant Christian regime in the centre of the Iberian Peninsula. In Morocco it was neither the fervour of warriors nor Shi'ite solidarity nor Timurid restoration that motivated the formation of a state; rather, it was a very old form of legitimacy that had proved to be especially powerful in Africa—that of the sharifs, descendants of Muhammad. It had last been relied on with the Idrisids; now the sharifs were often associated with Sufi holy men, known as *marabouts*. It was one such Sufi, Sidi Barakat, who legitimated the Sa'di family of sharifs as leaders of a jihad that expelled the Portuguese and established an independent state (1511–1603) strong enough to expand far to the south. Meanwhile, the greatest Muslim kingdom of the Sudan, Songhai, was expanding northward, and its growing control of major trade routes into Morocco provoked Moroccan interference. Invaded in 1591, Songhai was ruled as a Moroccan vassal for 40 years, during which time Morocco itself was experiencing political confusion and instability. Morocco was reunited under Isma'il (ruled 1672–1727), an 'Alawite sharif. A holy family of Sijilmassa, the 'Alawites were brought to power by Arab tribal support, which they eventually had to replace with a costly army of black slaves. Like the Sa'dis, they were legitimated in two ways: by the recognition of leading Sufis and by the special spiritual quality (*barakah*) presumed to have passed to them by virtue of their descent from the Prophet through 'Ali. Although they were not Shi'ites, they cultivated charismatic leadership that undermined the power of the *ulama* to use the Shari'ah against them. They also recognized the limits of their authority as absolute monarchs, dividing their realm into the area of authority and the area of no authority (where many of the Amazigh tribes lived). Thus, the Moroccan sharifs solved the universal problems of legitimacy, loyalty, and control in a way tailored to their own situation.

While the Sa'di dynasty was ruling in Morocco but long before its incursions into the Sahara, a number of small Islamic states were strung from one end of the Sudanic region to the other: Senegambia, Songhai, Aïr, Mossi, Nupe, Hausa, Kanem-Bornu, Darfur, and Funj. Islam had come to these areas along trade and pilgrimage routes, especially through the efforts of a number of learned teaching-trading families such as the Kunta. Ordinarily the ruling elites became Muslim first, employing the skills of Arab immigrants, traders, or travelers, and taking political and commercial advantage of the Arabic language and the Shari'ah without displacing indigenous religious practices or legitimating principles. By the 16th century the Muslim states of the Sudanic belt were in contact not only with the major Muslim centres of the Maghrib and Egypt but also with each other through an emerging trans-Sudanic pilgrimage route. Furthermore, Islam had by then become well enough established to provoke efforts at purification comparable to the Almoravid movement of the 11th century. Sometimes these efforts were gradualist and primarily educational, as was the case with the enormously influential Egyptian scholar al-Suyuti (1445–1505). His works, read by many West African Muslims for centuries after his death, dealt with numerous subjects, including the coming of the *mahdi* to restore justice and strengthen Islam. He also wrote letters to Muslim scholars and rulers in West Africa more than 2,000 miles (3,200 km) away, explaining the Shari'ah and encouraging its careful observance.

Other efforts to improve the observance of Islam were more militant. Rulers might forcibly insist on an end to certain non-Muslim practices, as did Muhammad Rumfa (ruled 1463–99) in the Hausa city-state of Kano, or Muhammad I Askia, the greatest ruler of Songhai (ruled 1493–1528). Often, as in the case of both of these rulers, militance was encouraged by an aggressive reformist scholar like al-Maghili (flourished 1492), whose writings detailed the conditions that would justify a jihad against Muslims who practiced their faith inadequately. Like many reformers, al-Maghili identified himself as a *mujaddid*, a figure expected to appear around the turn of each Muslim century. (The 10th century AH began in 1494 CE.) To the east in Ethiopia, an actual jihad was carried out by Ahmad Grañ (c. 1506–43), in the name of opposition to the Christian regime and purification of "compromised" Islam. Farther to the east, a conquest of Christian Nubia by Arab tribes of Upper Egypt resulted in the conversion of the pagan Funj to Islam and the creation of a major Muslim kingdom there. Although most indigenous West African scholars looked to foreigners for inspiration, a few began to chart their own course. In Timbuktu, where a rich array of Muslim learning was available, one local scholar and member of a Tukulor learned family, Ahmad

Baba, was writing works that were of interest to North African Muslims. Local histories written in Arabic also survive, such as the *Ta'rikh al-fattash* (written by several generations of the Kati family, from 1519 to 1665), a chronological history of Songhai, or al-Sa'di's *Ta'rikh al-Sudan* (completed in 1655). By the end of the period of consolidation and expansion, Muslims in the Sudanic belt were being steadily influenced by North African Islam but were also developing distinctive traditions of their own.

INDIAN OCEAN ISLAM

A similar relationship was simultaneously developing across another "sea," the Indian Ocean, which tied South and Southeast Asian Muslims to East African and south Arabian Muslims the way the Sahara linked North African and Sudanic Muslims. Several similarities are clear: the alternation of advance and retreat, the movement of outside influences along trade routes, and the emergence of significant local scholarship. There were differences too: Indian Ocean Muslims had to cope with the Portuguese threat and to face Hindus and Buddhists more than pagans, so that Islam had to struggle against sophisticated and refined religious traditions that possessed written literature and considerable political power.

The first major Muslim state in Southeast Asia, Aceh, was established around 1524 in northern and western Sumatra in response to more than a decade of Portuguese advance. Under Sultan Iskandar Muda (ruled 1607–37), Aceh reached the height of its prosperity and importance in the Indian Ocean trade, encouraging Muslim learning and expanding Muslim adherence. By the end of the 17th century, Aceh's Muslims were in touch with major intellectual centres to the west, particularly in India and Arabia, just as West African Muslims were tied to centres across

The Great Mosque, Palembang, Sumatra, Indon. Richard Allen Thompson

the Sahara. Because they could draw on many sources, often filtered through India, Sumatran Muslims may have been exposed to a wider corpus of Muslim learning than Muslims in many parts of the heartland. Aceh's scholarly disputes over Ibn al-'Arabi were even significant enough to attract the attention of a leading Medinan, Ibrahim al-Kurani, who in 1640 wrote a response. The same kind of naturalization and indigenization of Islam that was taking place in Africa was also taking place elsewhere; for example, 'Abd al-Ra'uf of Singkel, after studying in Arabia from about 1640 to 1661, returned home, where he made the first "translation" of the Qur'an into Malay, a language that was much enriched during this period by Arabic script and vocabulary. This phenomenon extended even to China. Liu Zhi, a scholar born around 1650 in Nanjing, created serious Islamicate literature in Chinese, including works of philosophy and law.

In the early 17th century another Muslim commercial power emerged when its ruler, the prince of Tallo, converted. Macassar (now Makassar) became an active centre for Muslim competition with the Dutch into the third quarter of the 17th century, when its greatest monarch, Hasan al-Din (ruled 1631–70), was forced to cede his independence. Meanwhile, however, a serious Islamic presence was developing in Java, inland as well as on the coasts; by the early 17th century the first inland Muslim state in Southeast Asia, Mataram, was established. There Sufi holy men performed a missionary function similar to that being performed in Africa. Unlike the more seriously Islamized states in Sumatra, Mataram suffered, as did its counterparts in West Africa, from its inability to suppress indigenous beliefs to the satisfaction of the more conservative *ulama*. Javanese Muslims, unlike those in Sumatra, would have to struggle for centuries to negotiate the confrontation between Hindu and Muslim cultures. Their situation underscores a major theme of Islamicate history through the period of consolidation and expansion—that is, the repeatedly demonstrated absorptive capacity of Muslim societies, a capacity that was soon to be challenged in unprecedented ways.

CHAPTER 7

ISLAMIC HISTORY FROM 1683 TO THE PRESENT: REFORM, DEPENDENCY, AND RECOVERY

The history of modern Islam has often been explained in terms of the impact of "the West." From this perspective, the 18th century was a period of degeneration and a prelude to European domination, symbolized by Napoleon's conquest of Egypt in 1798. Yet it is also possible to argue that the period of Western domination was merely an interlude in the ongoing development of indigenous styles of modernization. In order to resolve this question, it is necessary to begin the "modern" period with the 18th century, when activism and revival were present throughout Islamdom. The three major Muslim empires did experience a decline during the 18th century, as compared with their own earlier power and with the rising powers in Europe, but most Muslims were not yet aware that Europe was partly to blame. Similar decline had occurred many times before, a product of the inevitable weaknesses of the military conquest state turned into centralized absolutism, overdependence on continuous expansion, weakening of training for rule, the difficulty of maintaining efficiency and loyalty in a large and complex royal household and army, and the difficulty of maintaining sufficient revenues for an increasingly lavish court life. Furthermore, population increased, as it did almost everywhere in the 18th-century world, just as inflation and expensive reform reduced income to central governments. Given the insights of Ibn Khaldun, however, one might have expected a new group with a fresh sense of cohesiveness to restore political strength.

Had Muslims remained on a par with all other societies, they might have revived. But by the 18th century one particular set of societies in western Europe had developed an economic and social system capable of transcending the 5,000-year-old limitations of the agrarian-based settled world as defined by the Greeks (who called it *Oikoumene*). Unlike most of the lands of Islamdom, those societies were rich in natural resources (especially the fossil fuels that could supplement human and animal power) and poor in space for expansion. Cut off by Muslims from controlling land routes from the East, European explorers had built on and surpassed Muslim seafaring technology to compete in the southern seas and discover new sea routes—and, accidentally, a new source of wealth in the Americas. In Europe, centralized absolutism, though an ideal, had not been the success it was in Islamdom. Emerging from the landed classes rather than from the cities, it had benefited from and been constrained by independent urban commercial classes. In Islamdom, the power of merchants had been inhibited by imperial over-taxation of local private enterprise, appropriation of the benefits of trade, and the privileging of foreign traders through agreements known as the Capitulations.

In Europe independent financial and social resources promoted an unusual freedom for technological experimentation and, consequently, the technicalization of other areas of society as well. Unlike previous innovations in the *Oikoumene*, Europe's technology could not easily be diffused to societies that had not undergone the prerequisite fundamental social and economic changes. Outside Europe, gradual assimilation of the "new," which had characterized change and cultural diffusion for 5,000 years, had to be replaced by hurried imitation, which proved enormously disorienting. This combination of innovation and imitation produced an unprecedented and persisting imbalance among various parts of the *Oikoumene*. Muslims' responses paralleled those of other "non-Western" peoples but were often filtered through and expressed in peculiarly Islamic or Islamicate symbols and motifs. The power of Islam as a source of public values had already waxed and waned many times; it intensified in the 18th and 19th centuries, receded in the early 20th century, and surged again after the mid-20th century. Thus European colonizers appeared in the midst of an ongoing process that they greatly affected but did not completely transform.

PRE-COLONIAL REFORM AND EXPERIMENTATION (1683 TO 1818)

From the mid-17th century through the 18th and early 19th centuries certain Muslims expressed an awareness of internal weakness in their societies. In some areas, Muslims were largely unaware of the rise of Europe; in others, such as India, Sumatra, and Java, the 18th century actually brought European control. Responses to decline, sometimes official and sometimes unofficial, sometimes Islamizing and sometimes Europeanizing, fell into two categories, as the following examples demonstrate.

In some areas leaders attempted to revive existing political systems. In Iran, for example, attempts at restoration combined military and religious reform. About 1730 a Turk from Khorasan named Nadr Qoli Beg reorganized the Safavid army in the name of the Safavid shah, whom he replaced with himself in 1736. Taking the title Nadir Shah, he extended the borders of the Safavid state farther than ever; he even defeated the Ottomans and may have aspired to be the leader of all Muslims. To this end he made overtures to neighbouring rulers, seeking their recognition by trying to represent Iranian Shi'ism as a *madhhab* (school of Islamic law) alongside the Sunni *madhhabs*. After he was killed in 1747, however, his reforms did not survive and his house disintegrated. Karim Khan Zand, a general from Shiraz, ruled in the name of the Safavids but did not restore real power to the shah. By the time the Qajars (1779–1925) managed to resecure Iran's borders, reviving Safavid legitimacy was impossible.

In the Ottoman Empire restoration involved selective imitation of things European. Its first phase, from 1718 to 1730, is known as the Tulip Period because of the cultivation by the wealthy of a Perso-Turkish flower then popular in Europe. Experimentation with European manners and tastes was matched by experimentation with European military technology. Restoration depended on reinvigorating the military, the key to earlier Ottoman success, and Christian Europeans were hired for the task. After Nadir Shah's defeat of the Ottoman army, this first phase of absolutist restoration ended, but the pursuit of European fashion had become a permanent element in Ottoman life. Meanwhile, central power continued to weaken, especially in the area of international commerce. The certificates of protection that had accompanied the Capitulations arrangements for foreign nationals were extended to non-Muslim Ottoman subjects, who gradually oriented themselves toward their foreign associates. The Ottoman state was further weakened by the recognition, in the disastrous Treaty of Kücük Kaynarca (1774), of the Russian tsar as protector of the Ottoman's Greek Orthodox *millet*. A second stage of absolutist restoration occurred under Selim III, who became sultan in the first year of the French Revolution and ruled until 1807. His military and political reforms, referred to as the new order (*nizam-ı cedid*), went beyond the Tulip Period in making use of things European; for example, the enlightened monarch, as exemplified by Napoleon himself, became an Ottoman ideal. There, as in Egypt under Muhammad 'Ali (reigned 1805–48), the famed corps of Janissaries, the elite troops that had been a source of Ottoman strength was destroyed and replaced with European-trained troops.

In other areas, leaders envisioned or created new social orders that were self-consciously Islamic. The growing popularity of Westernization and a decreasing reliance on Islam as a source of public values was counterbalanced in many parts of Islamdom by all sorts of Islamic activism, ranging from educational reform to jihad. "Islamic" politics were often marked by an oppositional quality that drew on long-standing traditions of skepticism about government. Sufism could play very different roles. In the form of renovated *tariqah*s, communities of followers gathered around sheikhs (or *pir*s, "teachers"), it could support reform and stimulate a consciousness marked by Pan-Islamism (the idea that Islam can be the basis of a unified political and cultural order). Sufis often encouraged the study of Hadith, which they used to establish a model for spiritual and moral reconstruction and to invalidate many unacceptable traditional or customary Islamic practices. Sufi *tariqah*s provided interregional communication and contact and an indigenous form of social organization that in some cases led to the founding of a dynasty, as with the Libyan monarchy.

Sufism could also be condemned as a source of degeneracy. The most famous and influential militant anti-Sufi

movement arose in the Arabian Peninsula and called itself
al-Muwahhidun ("the Unitarians"), although it came to be
known as Wahhabism, after its founder, Muhammad ibn
'Abd al-Wahhab (1703–92). Inspired by Ibn Taymiyyah, Ibn
al-Wahhab argued that the Qur'an and Sunnah could provide the basis for a reconstruction of Islamic society out
of the degenerate form in which it had come to be practiced. Islam itself was not an inhibiting force; "traditional"
Islam was. Far from advocating the traditional, the
Wahhabis argued that what had become traditional had
strayed very far from the fundamental, which can always
be found in the Qur'an and Sunnah. The traditional they
associated with blind imitation (*taqlid*); reform, with
making the pious personal effort (*ijtihad*) necessary to
understand the fundamentals. Within an Islamic context
this type of movement was not conservative because it
sought not to conserve what had been passed down but to
renew what had been abandoned. The Wahhabi movement attracted the support of a tribe in the Najd led by
Muhammad ibn Sa'ud. Although the first state produced
by this alliance did not last, it laid the foundations for the
existing Saudi state in Arabia and inspired similar activism
elsewhere down to the present day.

In West Africa a series of activist movements appeared
from the 18th century into the 19th. There as in Arabia,
Islamic activism was directed less at non-Muslims than at
Muslims who had gone astray. As in many of Islamdom's
outlying areas, emergent groups of indigenous educated,
observant Muslims, such as the Tukulor, were finding the
casual, syncretistic, opportunistic nature of official Islam
to be increasingly intolerable. Such Muslims were inspired
by reformist scholars from numerous times and places
(including al-Ghazali, al-Suyuti, and al-Maghili), by a theory of jihad comparable to that of the Wahhabis, and by
expectations of a *mujaddid* at the turn of the Islamic

century in AH 1200 (1785 CE). In what is now northern Nigeria, the discontent of the 1780s and 1790s erupted in 1804, when the Fulani mystic, philosopher, and revolutionary reformer Usman dan Fodio (1754–1817) declared a jihad against the Hausa rulers. Others followed, among them Muhammad al-Jaylani in Aïr, Shehuh Ahmadu Lobbo in Macina, al-Hajj 'Umar Tal (a member of the reformist Tijani *tariqah*) in Fouta Djallon, and Samory in the Malinke (Mandingo) states. Jihad activity continued for a century; it again became millennial near the turn of the next Muslim century in AH 1300 (1882 CE), as the need to resist European occupation became more urgent. For example, Muhammad Ahmad declared himself to be the *mahdi* in the Sudan in 1881.

In the Indian Ocean area, Islamic activism was more often intellectual and educational. Its best exemplar was Shah Wali Allah of Delhi (1702/3–62), the spiritual ancestor of many later Indian Muslim reform movements. During his lifetime the collapse of Muslim political power was painfully evident. He tried to unite the Muslims of India, not around Sufism as Akbar had tried to do, but around the Shari'ah. Like Ibn Taymiyyah, he understood the Shari'ah to be based on firm sources—the Qur'an and Sunnah—that could with pious effort be applied to present circumstances. Once again the study of Hadith provided a rich array of precedents and inspired a positive spirit of social reconstruction akin to that of the Prophet Muhammad.

THE RISE OF BRITISH COLONIALISM TO THE END OF THE OTTOMAN EMPIRE

The many efforts to revive and resist were largely unsuccessful. By 1818 British hegemony over India was complete, and many other colonies and mandates followed between then and the aftermath of World War I. Not all Muslim territories were colonized, but nearly all experienced some kind of dependency, be it psychological, political, technological, cultural, or economic. Perhaps only the Saudi regime in the central parts of the Arabian Peninsula could be said to have escaped any kind of dependency; but even there oil exploration, begun in the 1930s, brought European interference. In the 19th century Westernization and Islamic activism coexisted and competed. By the turn of the 20th century secular ethnic nationalism had become the most common mode of protest in Islamdom, but the spirit of Islamic reconstruction was also kept alive, either in conjunction with secular nationalism or in opposition to it.

In the 19th-century Ottoman Empire, selective Westernization coexisted with a reconsideration of Islam. The program of reform known as the Tanzimat, which was in effect from 1839 to 1876, aimed to emulate European law and administration by giving all Ottoman subjects, regardless of religious confession, equal legal standing and by limiting the powers of the monarch. In the 1860s a group known as the Young Ottomans tried to identify the basic principles of European liberalism—and even love of nation—with Islam itself. In Iran the Qajar shahs brought in a special "Cossack Brigade," trained and led by Russians, while at the same time the Shi'ite *mujtahid*s viewed the decisions of their spiritual leader as binding on all Iranian Shi'ites and declared themselves to be independent of the shah. (One Shi'ite revolt, that of the Bab [died 1850], led to a whole new religion, the Baha'i faith.) Like the Young Ottomans, Shi'ite religious leaders came to identify with constitutionalism in opposition to the ruler.

Islamic protest often took the form of jihad against Europeans: by Southeast Asians against the Dutch; by the

Sanusi *tariqah* over Italian control in Libya; by the Mahdist movement in the Sudan; or by the Salihi *tariqah* in Somalia, led by Sayyid Muhammad ibn 'Abd Allah Hasan, who was nicknamed the Mad Mullah by Europeans. Sometimes religious leaders, such as those of the Shi'ites in Iran (1905–11), took part in constitutional revolutions. Underlying much of this activity was a Pan-Islamic sentiment that drew on very old conceptions of the *ummah* as the ultimate solidarity group for Muslims. Three of the most prominent Islamic reconstructionists were Jamal al-Din al-Afghani, his Egyptian disciple Muhammad 'Abduh, and the Indian poet Sir Muhammad Iqbal. All warned against the blind pursuit of Westernization, arguing that blame for the weaknesses of Muslims lay not with Islam but rather with Muslims themselves, because they had lost touch with the progressive spirit of social, moral, and intellectual reconstruction that had made early Islamicate civilization one of the greatest in human history. Although al-Afghani, who taught and preached in many parts of Islamdom, acknowledged that organization by nationality might be necessary, he viewed it as inferior to Muslim identity. He further argued that Western technology could advance Muslims only if they retained and cultivated their own spiritual and cultural heritage. He pointed out that at one time Muslims had been intellectual and scientific leaders in the world, identifying a golden age under the 'Abbasid caliphate and pointing to the many contributions Muslims had made to the West. Like al-Afghani, Iqbal assumed that without Islam Muslims could never regain the strength they had possessed when they were a vital force in the world, united in a single international community and unaffected by differences of language or ethnos. This aggressive recovery of the past became a permanent theme of Islamic reconstruction. In many regions of Islamdom the movement known as Salafiyyah also identified with an ideal time in history, that of the "pious ancestors" (*salaf*) in the early Muslim state of Muhammad and his companions, and advocated past-oriented change to bring present-day Muslims up to the progressive standards of an earlier ideal. In addition to clearly Islamic thinkers, there were others, such as the Egyptian Mustafa Kamil, whose nationalism was not simply secular. Kamil saw Egypt as simultaneously European, Ottoman, and Muslim. The Young Turk Revolution of 1908 was followed by a period in which similarly complex views of national identity were discussed in the Ottoman Empire.

ISLAM AND NATIONALISM IN THE AGE OF GLOBALIZATION (THE EARLY 20TH CENTURY TO THE PRESENT)

REFORM AND REVIVAL IN THE COLONIAL PERIOD

The tension between Islamic and national identification remained crucial for Muslims at the start of the 20th century. In countries under Western colonial rule, the struggle for national independence often went hand in hand with an effort by reformist intellectuals to recover the authentic message of the original Muslim community. Between the two World Wars, two distinct interpretations of Islam emerged from the Salafiyyah movement.

One interpretation, drawing upon Pan-Islamism, politicized Islam by taking its scriptures to be the proper foundation of the social and political order. The writings of the Syrian Egyptian scholar Muhammad Rashid Rida (1865–1935) provided a basis for such an interpretation. Like earlier reformers, Rashid Rida viewed the cult of saints (the veneration of holy figures) as a corruption of Islam, and he sought a renovated religion that would be grounded in and faithful to the religion's early scriptures. He insisted, however, that such a renovation entailed the implementation of Islamic precepts in social and political life. Rashid Rida considered the 1924 dissolution of the Ottoman caliphate to be a traumatic event because it marked the end (in his eyes) of a religious and political entity that had existed since the death of the Prophet. Yet he hailed the seizure of Mecca by the Arabian tribal leader 'Abd al-'Aziz ibn Sa'ud that same year. This led to the founding in 1932 of the modern state of Saudi Arabia, which Rashid Rida considered a model Islamic state.

Rashid Rida was widely influential among Muslims who were hoping for a wholly Islamic society. For example, his thought inspired Hasan al-Banna' (1906–49), who founded the militant organization the Muslim Brotherhood in Egypt in 1928. The Brotherhood later influenced other militant Islamic groups.

In contrast to these thinkers, the Egyptian reformer 'Ali 'Abd al-Raziq (1888–1966) claimed that Islam could not be the basis of a society's political system because Muhammad was the last of the prophets. After direct revelation from God ended with Muhammad, al-Raziq maintained, Islam could have only a spiritual function; the use of religion for political aims could not be legitimate. The caliphate was merely a political construction and not an essential aspect of Islam. Its disappearance with the end of the Ottoman Empire, therefore, was not a matter of concern. Henceforward, each predominantly Muslim country would be free to determine its own political system. Although the great majority of the *ulama* rejected 'Abd al-Raziq's view, secular elites blended it with a liberal conception of society that regarded religion as only one of several cultural elements rather than as a comprehensive code of life. In the countries of the Maghrib (the North African Mediterranean), this understanding of Islam inspired visions of uniting the religion with Amazigh,

RASHID RIDA

Muhammad Rashid Rida (1865–1935) was a Syrian scholar who helped formulate an intellectual response to the problem of reconciling Islamic heritage with the modern world.

Rashid Rida was educated according to traditional forms of Muslim learning—the sciences of the Islamic religion and the Arabic language. He was profoundly influenced in his early years by the writings of Muhammad 'Abduh and Jamal al-Din al-Afghani, Muslim reformist and nationalist thinkers, and he became 'Abduh's biographer and the leading exponent and defender of his ideas. Rashid Rida founded the newspaper *al-Manar* in 1898 and published it throughout his life. To a limited extent, he also participated in the political affairs of Syria and Egypt.

He was concerned with the backwardness of the Muslim countries, which he believed resulted from a neglect of the true principles of Islam. He believed that these principles could be found in the teachings of the Prophet Muhammad and in the practices of the first generation of Muslims, before corruptions began to spread among the religious practices of the faithful (*c.* 655). He was convinced that Islam, as a body of teachings correctly understood, contained all the principles necessary for happiness in this world and the hereafter, and that positive effort to improve the material basis of the community was of the essence of Islam.

Rashid Rida urged Arabs to emulate the scientific and technological progress made by the West. In the political affairs of the Muslim community, he wanted rulers to respect the authority of the men of religion and to consult with them in the formulation of governmental policies. Here he showed his tendency to assimilate practices of traditional Islam into the forms of modern societies. Consultation had never been institutionalized in traditional Islam, but he equated it with modern parliamentary government. He sanctioned the bending of Islam to fit the demands of modern times in other important respects; for example, the Prophet had forbidden the taking of interest, but Rashid Rida believed that, to combat effectively the penetration of Western capitalism, Muslims had to accept the policy of taking interest.

To realize a political and cultural revival, Rashid Rida saw the need to unify the Muslim community. He advocated the establishment of a true caliph, who would be the supreme interpreter of Islam and whose prestige would enable him to guide Muslim governments in the directions demanded by an Islam adapted to the needs of modern society.

Arab, and Mediterranean cultures to create a single cultural identity. Similarly, in Egypt liberal intellectuals such as Taha Husayn (1889–1973) viewed their national culture as incorporating Islamic, Arabic, ancient Egyptian, and European elements.

The question of whether Islam should be the foundation of a national culture and politics dominated political discourse in Islamic countries throughout the 20th century and beyond. In particular, the political interpretation of Islam inspired resistance to Western acculturation. Religious scholars and intellectuals such as 'Abd al-Hamid ben Badis (1899–1940), founder in 1931 of the Association of Algerian Muslim Ulama, and Muhammad 'Allal al-Fasi (1910–74) in Morocco reconceived the identity of their countries in Islamic terms and played significant roles in nationalist movements until independence was achieved. Between the two World Wars, these scholars established several Islamic private schools offering Arabic-language instruction for boys and girls. Islamic intellectuals and movements often put their educational endeavours at the centre of their projects to bring Islam into agreement with their times. Thus, the question of the transmission of Islamic knowledge versus secular and Westernized education became crucial. Yet not all Islamic thinkers viewed the two systems of education as incompatible. Some argued that they should be integrated and could complement each other. The Indonesian Nahdatul Ulama, for instance, favoured a system of Islamic schooling along modernized lines that would integrate religious and secular knowledge.

NATIONALISM: POSTCOLONIAL STATES AND ISLAM

Later in the 20th century, colonized Muslim societies (except Palestine) gradually achieved political independence and built new states. Many of these states adopted a "Muslim" identity that they interpreted in various ways and implemented within such domains as law, education, and moral conduct. Two states, though established in societies that had not been colonized, exemplified contrasting paradigms. In 1924 the Turkish military officer Mustafa Kemal, taking the name Atatürk ("Father of the Turks"), brought a formal end to the Ottoman caliphate. Maintaining that Islam had contributed to the backwardness of Turkish society and that a modern country must be founded upon science and reason rather than religion, Atatürk claimed to relegate Islam to the private sphere. This brand of secularist government also controlled the public expression of Islam and did not separate state and religion. In Saudi Arabia, on the other hand, the state regulated public life according to Islamic norms, using a rigorous interpretation of Shari'ah.

In Egypt, which became a constitutional monarchy after 1922 (though it was under colonial control until 1952), the question of the relation between state and Islam generated fierce political controversies between secularists and those who interpreted Islam as a system of government. Among the latter, the Muslim Brotherhood grew from a grassroots organization into a mass movement that provided key popular support for the 1952 Revolution of the Free Officers, a military coup led by Col. Gamal Abdel Nasser that ousted the monarchy. Similar movements in Palestine, Syria, Jordan, and North Africa, the politicized heirs of earlier reformist intellectual trends, later emerged as significant actors in their respective political scenes. It was not until the end of the 1960s, however, that they became strong enough to pose a serious political challenge to their countries' authoritarian regimes.

MUSLIM BROTHERHOOD

The Muslim Brotherhood (Arabic: al-Ikhwan al-Muslimun) is a religio-political organization founded in 1928 at Ismailia, Egypt, by Hasan al-Banna'. It advocated a return to the Qur'an and the Hadith as guidelines for a healthy, modern Islamic society. The Brotherhood spread rapidly throughout Egypt, the Sudan, Syria, Palestine, Lebanon, and North Africa. Although figures of Brotherhood membership are variable, it is estimated that at its height in the late 1940s it may have had some 500,000 members.

Initially centred on religious and educational programs, the Muslim Brotherhood was seen as providing much-needed social services, and in the 1930s its membership grew swiftly. In the late 1930s the Brotherhood began to politicize its outlook, and, as an opponent of Egypt's ruling Wafd party, during World War II it organized popular protests against the government. An armed branch organized in the early 1940s was subsequently linked to a number of violent acts, including bombings and political assassinations, and it appears that the armed element of the group began to escape Hasan al-Banna''s control. The Brotherhood responded to the government's attempts to dissolve the group by assassinating Prime Minister Mahmud Fahmi al-Nuqrashi in December 1948. Hasan al-Banna' himself was assassinated shortly thereafter; many believe his death was at the behest of the government.

With the advent of the revolutionary regime in Egypt in 1952, the Brotherhood retreated underground. An attempt to assassinate Egyptian Pres. Gamal Abdel Nasser in Alexandria on Oct. 26, 1954, led to the Muslim Brotherhood's forcible suppression. Six of its leaders were tried and executed for treason, and many others were imprisoned. Among those imprisoned was writer Sayyid Qutb, who authored a number of books during the course of his imprisonment; among these works was *Signposts in the Road*, which would become a template for modern Sunni militancy. Although he was released from prison in 1964, he was arrested again the following year and executed shortly thereafter. In the 1960s and 1970s the Brotherhood's activities remained largely clandestine.

In the 1980s the Muslim Brotherhood experienced a renewal as part of the general upsurge of religious activity in Islamic countries. The Brotherhood's new adherents aimed to reorganize society and government according to Islamic doctrines, and they were vehemently anti-Western. An uprising by the Brotherhood in the Syrian city of Hamah in February 1982 was crushed by the government of Hafiz al-Assad at a cost of perhaps 25,000 lives. The Brotherhood revived in Egypt and Jordan in the same period, and beginning in the late 1980s it emerged to compete in legislative elections in those countries.

In Egypt the participation of the Muslim Brotherhood in parliamentary elections there in the 1980s was followed by its boycott of the elections of 1990, when it joined most of the country's opposition in protesting electoral strictures. Although the group itself remained formally banned, in the 2000 elections Brotherhood supporters running as independent candidates were able to win 17 seats, making it the largest opposition bloc in the parliament. In 2005, again running as independents, the Brotherhood and its supporters captured 88 seats in spite of efforts by Pres. Hosni Mubarak's administration to restrict voting in the group's strongholds. Its unexpected success in 2005 was met with additional restrictions and arrests, and the Brotherhood opted to boycott the 2008 elections.

ISLAMIST MOVEMENTS FROM THE 1960S

With the defeat in June 1967 of the Arab states by Israel in the Six-Day (June) War, socialist and Pan-Arab ideologies declined in the Islamic world while political Islam emerged as a public force. Egypt, which had been under the influence of the Soviet Union since the mid-1950s, withdrew from military and other treaties with the Soviets in the 1970s under Pres. Anwar el-Sadat. A new alliance between Egypt and Saudi Arabia, fostered by economic assistance to Egypt from Saudi Arabia and other oil-producing Persian Gulf states, altered the geopolitical map of Islam and led to new religious dynamics. In 1962 the Saudi regime established the Muslim World League in Mecca with the participation of Muslim scholars and intellectuals from all over the world. The league, whose mission was to unify Muslims and promote the spread of Islam, opened offices in the Islamic world in the 1960s and in the West in subsequent decades. With financial assistance as well as religious guidance from the league, new Islamic organizations were created by revivalist movements in the Islamic world and by immigrant Muslim communities in Europe and America.

During this period Islamist movements, which insisted that society and government should conform to Islamic values, began to openly criticize state control of Islam in their countries and condemned their governments' minimalist interpretations of Islamic norms. These movements were diverse from the start and did not reach public prominence until 1979, when an Islamic state was founded in Iran through revolution. The Iranian Revolution was influenced by Third Worldism (a political ideology emphasizing the economic gap between developed Western states and countries in other parts of the world) and by Marxism. Particularly important were the vehement critique of Western influence developed by Jalal Al-e Ahmad

Iranian soldiers visit Ayatollah Khomeini's tomb outside Tehran during a ceremony marking the 30th anniversary of Khomeini's return from exile. Atta Kenare/AFP/Getty Images

(1923–69) and the Marxist-oriented Islamic reformism promoted by 'Ali Shari'ati (1933–77). The revolution's leader, Ayatollah Ruhollah Khomeini (1900–89), emphasized the themes of defending the disinherited (referred to by the Qur'anic word *mustadh'afin*) and resisting "Westoxification" (Farsi: *gharbzadegi*), a concept he borrowed from Al-e Ahmad and Shari'ati. He also coined and implemented in the new Islamic republic the concept of *velayat-e faqih*, or government by the Muslim jurist. The Iranian Revolution gave hope to many Islamist movements with similar programs by demonstrating the potential of Islam as a foundation for political mobilization and resistance. It further provided them with a blueprint for political action against governments that they believed had betrayed authentic Islam and grown corrupt and authoritarian. The Islamic republic of Iran also competed with Saudi Arabia at the international level for influence in the Middle East.

RUHOLLAH KHOMEINI

Ruhollah Khomeini (1900?–1989) was an Iranian Shi'ite cleric who led the revolution that overthrew Mohammad Reza Shah Pahlavi in 1979 and who was Iran's ultimate political and religious authority for the next 10 years.

Little is known of Khomeini's early life. There are various dates given for his birth, the most common being May 17, 1900, and Sept. 24, 1902. He was the grandson and son of mullahs, or Shi'ite religious leaders. When he was five months old, his father was killed on the orders of a local landlord. The young Khomeini was raised by his mother and aunt and then by his older brother. He was educated in various Islamic schools, and he settled in the city of Qom about 1922. About 1930 he adopted the name of his home town, Khomayn (also spelled Khomeyn or Khomen), as his surname. As a Shi'ite scholar and teacher, Khomeini produced numerous writings on Islamic philosophy, law, and ethics, but it was his outspoken opposition to Iran's ruler, Mohammad Reza Shah Pahlavi, his denunciations of Western influences, and his uncompromising advocacy of Islamic purity that won him his initial following in Iran. In the 1950s he was acclaimed as an ayatollah, or major religious leader, and by the early 1960s he had received the title of grand ayatollah, thereby making him one of the supreme religious leaders of the Shi'ite community in Iran.

In 1962–63 Khomeini spoke out against the shah's reduction of religious estates in a land-reform program and against the emancipation of women. His ensuing arrest sparked antigovernment riots, and, after a year's imprisonment, Khomeini was forcibly exiled from Iran on Nov. 4, 1964. He eventually settled in the Shi'ite holy city of Al-Najaf, Iraq, from where he continued to call for the shah's overthrow and the establishment of an Islamic republic in Iran.

From the mid-1970s Khomeini's influence inside Iran grew dramatically owing to mounting public dissatisfaction with the shah's regime. Iraq's ruler, Saddam Hussein, forced Khomeini to leave Iraq on Oct. 6, 1978. Khomeini then settled in Neauphle-le-Château, a suburb of Paris. From there his supporters relayed his tape-recorded messages to an increasingly aroused Iranian populace, and massive demonstrations, strikes, and civil unrest in late 1978 forced the departure of the shah from the country on Jan. 16, 1979. Khomeini arrived in Tehran in triumph on Feb. 1, 1979, and was acclaimed as the religious leader of Iran's revolution. He appointed a government four days later and on March 1 again took up residence in Qom. In December a referendum on a new constitution created an Islamic republic in Iran, with Khomeini named Iran's political and religious leader for life.

Khomeini himself proved unwavering in his determination to transform Iran into a theocratically ruled Islamic state. Iran's Shiʿite clerics largely took over the formulation of governmental policy, while Khomeini arbitrated between the various revolutionary factions and made final decisions on important matters requiring his personal authority. First his regime took political vengeance, with hundreds of people who had worked for the shah's regime reportedly executed. The remaining domestic opposition was then suppressed, its members being systematically imprisoned or killed. Iranian women were required to wear the veil, Western music and alcohol were banned, and the punishments prescribed by Islamic law were reinstated.

The main thrust of Khomeini's foreign policy was the complete abandonment of the shah's pro-Western orientation and the adoption of an attitude of unrelenting hostility toward both superpowers, the United States and the Soviet Union. In addition, Iran tried to export its brand of Islamic revivalism to neighbouring Muslim countries. Khomeini sanctioned Iranian militants' seizure of the U.S. embassy in Tehran (Nov. 4, 1979) and their holding of American diplomatic personnel as hostages for more than a year. He also refused to countenance a peaceful solution to the Iran-Iraq War, which had begun in 1980 and which he insisted on prolonging in the hope of overthrowing Saddam. Khomeini finally approved a cease-fire in 1988 that effectively ended the war.

Iran's course of economic development foundered under Khomeini's rule, and his pursuit of victory in the Iran-Iraq War ultimately proved futile. Khomeini, however, was able to retain his charismatic hold over Iran's Shiʿite masses, and he remained the supreme political and religious arbiter in the country until his death. His gold-domed tomb in Tehran's Behesht-e Zahra' cemetery has since become a shrine for his supporters. Ideologically, he is best remembered for having developed the concept of *velayat-e faqih* ("guardianship of the jurist") in a series of lectures and tracts first promulgated during exile in Iraq in the late 1960s and 1970s. Khomeini argued therein for the establishment of a theocratic government administered by Islamic jurists in place of corrupt secular regimes. The Iranian constitution of 1979 embodies articles upholding this concept of juristic authority.

Even before the Iranian Revolution, however, offshoots of the Muslim Brotherhood were radicalizing political Islam in other parts of the Islamic world. The most influential figure in this trend was the Egyptian author and Muslim Brotherhood member Sayyid Qutb. Qutb was a prolific writer while in prison and became an influential voice among Islamists until his execution by the regime of Nasser, then premier, in 1966. In his writings Qutb declared that the influence of Western-inspired secularism had caused his society to become un-Islamic and that a new vanguard of Muslims must bring it back to Islam. He saw this as the "solution" to the two failed secular ideologies, capitalism and communism, that had relegated religion to the periphery of government throughout the Islamic world. Thus, a new *ummah* under the sole sovereignty of Allah and his revealed word needed to be constituted, because secular nation-states—exemplified by Nasserist Egypt—had led only to barbarity. Qutb's ideology was also influenced by Abu al-Aʻla al-Mawdudi (1903–79), founder of the Islamic Assembly in British India in 1941, the first Islamic political party. The Islamic Assembly was reconfigured after the partition of Pakistan and India in 1947 in order to support the establishment of an Islamic state in Pakistan.

Beginning in the 1970s, a new generation of political activists who used violence and had no thorough Islamic education declared that their national leaders were "apostates" who had to be eliminated by force. In 1981 the radical group Egyptian Islamic Jihad assassinated el-Sadat for the 1979 peace treaty he had made with Israel, among other things. This trend was also present in North Africa and South Asia. In many cases these activists were violently repressed. In some instances conflicts with government authorities led to bloody civil wars, as in Algeria between 1992 and 2002, or to protracted armed struggles between military forces and Islamist groups, as in Egypt from the 1970s to the mid-1990s. This repression resulted in the exile of many Islamist activists to Europe and the Americas and led many others to join such military fronts as the Afghan Jihad.

THE MAINSTREAMING OF ISLAMIST MOVEMENTS

From the late 1970s, Islamist groups were the object of sustained worldwide media attention. Yet nonviolent groups received significantly less attention than the few groups that advocated the use of violence. Nonviolent Islamists often expressed their will to participate in legal electoral politics. This became possible in the 1990s, when authoritarian regimes—faced with serious socioeconomic crises and seeking to legitimize themselves in the eyes of the public—implemented policies of limited political liberalization, which in turn led to the participation of some Islamist movements in electoral politics and even to the co-optation of Islamist ideas by some governments.

The Muslim Brotherhood first engaged in electoral politics in Egypt in the 1980s and in Jordan as early as 1989.

In Morocco the Party of Justice and Development elected its first parliamentary representatives in 1997. In Indonesia the Prosperous Justice Party took part in legislative elections in 2004. Turkey allowed Islamists not only to participate in elections but also to govern at the national level. In 2002, Recep Tayyip Erdogan, chairman of the Justice and Development Party, which won a majority of seats in that year's general elections, formed a pragmatic Islamist government that cultivated diplomatic relations with Western powers.

In all these cases, mainstream opposition Islamist movements demonstrated their power to mobilize voters, a consequence of their social and charitable activism and their programs of good governance, especially their fight against government corruption. In contrast, such secular regimes as Fatah in the Palestinian territories and the government of Hosni Mubarak in Egypt were criticized by some segments of the citizenry as corrupt and repressive. In spite of their tendencies to speak about the universality of the Muslim community, Islamists remained nationalistic. Holding a conservative view of politics, they abandoned the revolutionary and utopian aspects of radical activism and instead struggled to moralize public and political life—e.g., by protesting "indecent" forms of entertainment and public behaviour and by insisting on accountability for political authorities. When they were allowed to govern, they rarely imposed Shari'ah-based legislation. Laws inspired by the Islamic legal tradition were implemented, however, in various forms in Iran after the 1979 revolution and in northern Sudan after 1983.

In countries that did not practice electoral politics, movements of opposition devised other means of protest and participation. In Saudi Arabia in 1993, a "Memorandum of Advice" was signed by more than 100 *ulama* and Islamists and was sent to Sheikh 'Abd al-'Aziz ibn Baz, the head of the Board of Senior Ulama and grand mufti of the state, to be passed on to the king. They requested an even greater role for the *ulama*, a comprehensive implementation of Shari'ah in Saudi society, social-welfare programs, respect for human rights, and a reorientation of Saudi foreign policy along "Islamic" lines.

Contemporary Islamist movements are polarized between two main trends. On the one hand, most movements are mainstream and pragmatic, seeking eventually to govern through participation in the political system and public debate. On the other hand, more-radical opposition groups reject electoral politics and seek revolutionary change, sometimes violently. Some groups alternate between these poles, choosing electoral participation or violence depending upon political circumstances, as in the case of Hamas in the West Bank and Gaza Strip and Hezbollah in Lebanon. In the first decade of the 21st century, some groups disconnected themselves from national politics in order to join transnational movements.

DIMENSIONS OF THE ISLAMIC REVIVAL

Various scholars have argued that Islamist movements emerged in reaction to the failure of state-led modernization projects and to general socioeconomic problems such as youth unemployment and poverty. Yet Islamist movements are not limited to poor countries or to disadvantaged, marginalized groups. In fact, members of these movements are generally highly educated, predominantly in secular fields, as a result of state-led modernization projects. In particular, mainstream Islamist parties are typically led by young men and women who are successful professionals with college or university degrees.

Scholars have also attempted to explain Islamism's rise as the direct result of the failure of Pan-Arabism in the

Arab Middle East and of secular nationalism in the Islamic world. As their Arab or national self-identifications break down, according to this view, people living in those countries turn to Islamism as a replacement. This is a misconception for two reasons. First, earlier forms of nationalism in Islamic countries were not devoid of religious ideas. Second, state institutions in those countries regulated the legal and public manifestations of Islam, in particular through their systems of public education.

In addition to becoming politicized in the hands of opposition movements and governments in the second half of the 20th century, Islam also followed a dynamic of revival that was deeply linked to sweeping educational, demographic, and social transformations. A young generation came of age in the 1960s, a time of rural exodus and urbanization, without having experienced colonial times. General access to education and the availability of printed Islamic literature also gave these young people an opportunity to build their own interpretations of Islam. Muslims could now study the Qur'an and the Sunnah without the mediation of the *ulama*, who represented a more institutionalized interpretation of Islam.

Technological innovations allowed some Islamic preachers to be heard or read, and even to develop followings, across the world. In the 1970s both the Ayatollah Khomeini and the Egyptian preacher Sheikh Kishk disseminated their speeches and sermons on audiocassettes. In the 1990s such new media as satellite television and the Internet began to offer faster means of access to ideas about Islam. In the late 1990s the Egyptian 'Amr Khalid became one of many popular preachers who reached a global audience. Through his Web site he disseminated advice on understanding and living Islam as a general ethics and on specific disciplines for achieving success and happiness in this world and in the afterlife.

Modernization in the Islamic world also encouraged Muslims to reevaluate gender relations. As Muslim women gained significant access to higher education and the job market, they became integral to public life in Muslim countries. In many instances, they sought to express their piety in the public sphere by drawing from and adapting Islamic tradition. One of the most widespread and (since the late 20th century) controversial expressions of piety among Muslim women was *hijab*, or the wearing of the veil. Veiling was never a uniform practice: elite women of earlier generations had unveiled, and the veils themselves ranged from a simple scarf to a full-body covering, depending upon country, culture, and economic class. In some Muslim countries—notably Iran and Saudi Arabia—veiling was required by law. Yet in many other countries and in the Muslim minority communities of Europe, Australia, and the United States, veiling was a massive voluntary phenomenon beginning in the 1970s. The veil remains a subject of political controversy in Western countries with large Muslim minorities, and throughout the Islamic world there is continuing debate about whether women should be veiled in public.

ISLAM AND GLOBALIZATION: THE AGE OF MOBILITY

Emigration of Muslims from the Middle East and South Asia accelerated after World War II and eventually produced large Muslim communities in the United States, Canada, and the countries of western Europe. While Islam was becoming politicized in the Islamic world, Western Muslims pondered how they could live and practice their religion in a non-Muslim context and whether full participation in Western culture and political life was possible, let alone desirable. These issues prompted the formation of numerous Muslim religious and cultural organizations in the West in the 1980s and '90s, including the Islamic Society of North America, the Union of Islamic Organizations in France, and the European Council for Fatwa and Research. These groups attempted to provide guidance to Muslims who wished to preserve their Islamic identity while contributing to the political and social life of their adoptive countries.

In the first decade of the 21st century, Western Muslims were still not fully integrated into their societies, and many suffered various forms of discrimination. Many also retained important links with their countries of origin through frequent travel and modern means of communication (e.g., the Internet). Second- and third-generation immigrants often had the opportunity to redefine Islamic practices and beliefs in opposition to their parents and grandparents, whose interpretations they considered too parochial, too strongly influenced by the culture of origin, or not close enough to a more abstract and universal type of Islam. While thus articulating a more personal religious identity, young Western Muslims (like young Muslims in other parts of the world) came to rely on religious authorities who were not associated with traditional Islamic institutions of learning. For this young generation, the fatwas (formal opinions on questions of Islamic doctrine) issued by such authorities became a crucially important source of answers to political and ethical questions. These fatwas, moreover, tended to represent Islam as a moral rather than a political community.

It was in this context of the Western institutionalization of Islam, and more generally of the transformation of Islam from a blueprint for a political and legal system into an ethics of conduct, that the September 11, 2001, attacks against the United States occurred. The attacks were staged by al-Qaeda, a radical Islamist organization

The Islamic Center of America mosque in Dearborn, Michigan, is seen here at sunset on 'Id al-Fitr, the feast marking the end of Ramadan. Bill Pugliano/ Getty Images

founded in the late 1980s by Osama bin Laden, a Saudi national. Bin Laden viewed the world as divided in a war between Muslims and "Crusaders and Zionists." Although the so-called "clash of civilizations" between Islam and the West was largely fictional, the term itself (coined in 1991 by the historian Bernard Lewis and popularized from 1993 by the political scientist Samuel P. Huntington) had a tremendously real power to mobilize public perceptions. The notion was reinforced both in the West and in the Islamic world by the September 11 attacks and the U.S.-led invasion of Afghanistan in 2001, the Iraq War in 2003, and the protracted inability of the international community to solve the conflict between the Palestinians and Israel.

Amid the ubiquitous language of global religious warfare, there were internal debates among Muslims about how the religious tradition should be interpreted, particularly as it concerned the use of violence, women's rights, and interfaith relations. Intellectuals such as Nurcholis Majid in Indonesia and Amina Wadud in the United States attempted to reclaim Islamic traditions by showing how Islam could accommodate liberal-democratic societies and ideas. Their visions of Islam also recognized full gender equality and individual freedom of expression. Meanwhile, such controversies as the banning of the veil in public schools in France and the publication in Denmark of cartoons caricaturing the Islamic faith (and particularly the Prophet Muhammad) became instantly global, transforming intellectual and political debates between Islam and other faiths and within Islam itself, challenging the modes of regulation of Islam in Muslim and non-Muslim countries alike.

Today, one-third of the world's Muslims live within minority communities. The rapid movement of Muslim immigrants to non-Muslim countries in modern times has meant a blurring of the distinction between Islam and the West. And although Islam has met with globalization before through migration, conquest, pilgrimage, and the use of Arabic language among far-flung learned classes, modern globalized Islam is altogether unique. It is a mass movement, not an elite one, and as emigration continues, the homeland left behind is not static but is itself greatly changed. The ummah, the community of believers, must be considered in abstract terms.

As Islam is deterritorialized—increasingly belonging not to a particular geographic place, culture, or society— the faith must now be redefined outside the context of a particular culture, and identities must be recast. Thus, the relationship between believers and their religion, and between Islam and society, continues to evolve. And as Muslims continue to face questions such as integration, exclusion, religious expression, and the relationship between religion and politics, such issues become ever increasingly global—and yet at the same time, local—in scope.

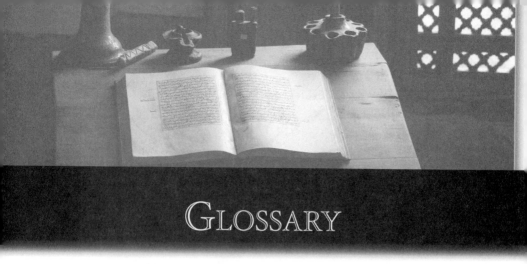

GLOSSARY

apostasy Abandonment of one's religion, principles, or cause.

Bedouin Arabic-speaking nomadic people of the Middle East.

caliph ("successor"), ruler of the Muslim community.

caravansary A public building (usually constructed outside the walls of a town or village) used for sheltering caravans and other travelers.

centrifugal Moving outward from the center.

coterminous Covering the same area.

eschatology Theology dealing with death and final matters.

eunuch A castrated male. In ancient China and the Middle East, eunuchs were hired as both harem guards and as high-ranking officials in royal courts.

florescence The state of blooming; flourishing.

hegemony Dominant influence by one nation over others, as a confederation.

heliocentricity The idea that the sun is the center of the solar system and all planets revolve around it.

imam The prayer leader of a mosque.

investiture Formal bestowal.

licentiousness Unrestrained by law or general morality.

lingua franca A language that is widely used as a means of communication among speakers of other languages.

madrasah A building or group of buildings used for teaching Islamic theology and religious law, usually including a mosque.

mosque A Muslim place of worship.

mullah An educated Muslim trained in traditional religious law and doctrine

palimpsest Something, such as a region, that has many different layers or aspects that can be seen beneath the surface.

pastoralist One whose life is based on the raising and herding of livestock.

peripatetic Itinerant; traveling.

sheikh A pre-Islamic title of respect borne by heads of religious orders, tribal chiefs, village headmen, learned men, etc.

supererogatory Going beyond the requirements of duty.

syncretism The attempted reconciliation of differing or opposing principles.

troika Any group of three acting equally in unison to exert influence, control, etc.

ummah The Muslim community.

zakat An obligatory alms tax required of Muslims; one of the five Pillars of Islam.

FOR FURTHER READING

Adamec, Ludwig. *Historical Dictionary of Islam*. Lanham, MD: Scarecrow Press, 2009.

Ahmed, Akbar S. *Islam Today*. London, England: I.B. Taurus, 1999.

Ansary, Tamim. *Destiny Disrupted: A History of the World Through Islamic Eyes*. New York, NY: PublicAffairs, 2009.

Armstrong, Karen. *Islam: A Short History*. New York, NY Modern Library, 2002.

Aslan, Reza. *No God but God: The Origins, Evolution and Future of Islam*. New York, NY: Random House, 2005.

Berry, Donald Lee. *Pictures of Islam*. Macon, GA: Mercer University Press, 2007.

Cleveland, William L. *A History of the Modern Middle East*. Boulder, CO: Westview Press, 2004.

Esposito, John L. *What Everyone Needs to Know About Islam*. New York, NY: Oxford University Press, 2002.

Hodgson, Marshall G.S. *The Venture of Islam*. 3 vols. Chicago, IL: University of Chicago Press, 1974–77.

Kennedy, Hugh. *The Great Arab Conquests: How the Spread of Islam Changed the World We Live In*. Philadelphia, PA: Da Capo Press, 2007.

Kennedy, Hugh. *The Prophet and the Age of the Caliphates: The Islamic Near East from the 6th to the 11th Century*. 2nd ed. White Plains, NY: Longman, 2004.

Lings, Martin. *Muhammad: His Life Based on the Earliest Sources*. Rochester, NY: Inner Traditions International, 2006.

Morris, Benny. *1948: A History of the First Arab-Israeli War*. New Haven, CT: Yale University Press, 2008.

Nasr, Seyyed Hossein. *Islam: Religion, History, and Civilization*. San Francisco, CA: HarperOne, 2003.

Rogerson, Barnaby. *The Heirs of Muhammed: Islam's First Century and the Origins of the Sunni-Shia Split*. Woodstock, NY: Overlook Press, 2007.

Sowell, Kirk H. *The Arab World: An Illustrated History*. New York, NY: Hippocrene Books, 2004.

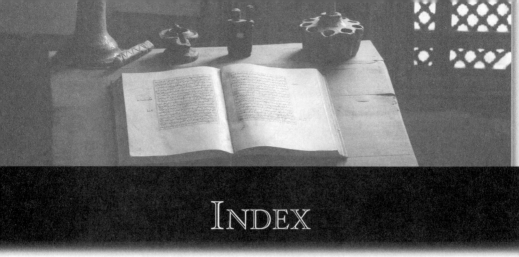

INDEX

A

'Abbas I, 168–169, 170, 172–173

'Abbasids, 15, 52, 74, 75–76, 77, 78, 80–85, 86, 89, 93–94, 95, 96, 97, 98, 99, 100, 105, 106, 113, 115, 121, 122, 133, 136, 139, 142, 192

'Abd al-Malik ibn Marwan, 65, 67–68, 69

'Abd al-Rahman I, 80, 95, 96

'Abd al-Rahman III, 95–97

'Abd al-Raziq, 'Ali, 194

'Abd al-Qadir al-Jilani, 126

'Abduh, Muhammad, 102, 192, 195

'Amr ibn al-'As, 58, 64

Abu 'Abd Allah al-Shi'i, 98–99

Abu al-'Abbas al-Saffah, 76

Abu al-Fadl, 173

Abu Bakr, 29, 40, 48, 49, 50, 51, 53, 55, 66

Abu Bakr ibn 'Umar, 148

Abu Hashim, 76

Abu Muslim, 75, 76, 80

Abu Talib, 13, 39

Abyssinians, 25, 27, 28, 32

al-'Adawiyyah, Rabi'ah, 108

al-Afghani, Jamal al-Din, 102, 192, 195

agrarian-based societies, rise of, 21–22

Ahmad, Muhammad, 190

Ahmad Baba, 180–181

Ahmad Grañ, 180

'A'ishah (Muhammad's wife), 48, 59, 63

Akbar, 172–174, 177, 190

'Alawites, 179

Al-e Ahmad, Jalal, 200–201

'Ali, 14, 59, 61–65, 75, 76, 77, 80, 99, 110, 165–166, 179

'Ali, Muhammad, 188

Almohads, 151–152

Almoravids, 148–151, 180

Alp-Arslan, 121, 122, 124, 125

Amazigh tribes, 66, 72, 97, 99, 146–147, 149, 152, 179, 194

al-Amin, 83, 87

Andalusia, Islamic dynasties in, 72–73, 89, 95–97, 147, 149, 151–152, 158

Arabian Peninsula, 25–28, 43, 58, 191

and trade routes, 12, 26, 30, 34

Arabic language, use of, 53, 67–68, 69, 70, 94, 114, 140, 146, 163, 195, 196, 212

Arabs, migration of, 133, 146–147

al-Ash'ari, Abu al-Hasan, 104–107
al-Ash'ari, Abu Musa, 64
Ash'arites, 150–151
Askia, Muhammad I, 180
al-Assad, Hafiz, 199
Aurangzeb, 174, 175, 176, 177
Avicenna (Ibn Sina), 114
Awliya', Nizam al-Din, 139
Axial Age, 20, 24–25, 37
Ayyubids, 101, 131, 133
al-Azhar University, 100, 101–102

B

Babak, 89
Babur, 15–16, 146, 170–172
Badr, Battle of, 43
Baghdad, 15, 80, 82, 85, 89, 93, 94, 100, 104, 105, 108, 109, 112–113, 116, 117, 121, 125, 126, 128, 136, 137, 149
Baha'i, 191
al-Banna', Hasan, 194, 198
Barakat, Sidi, 178
al-Basri, al-Hasan, 74–75, 107–108
Baybars I, 136
Bayezid (son of Süleyman), 162
Bayezid I, 143
Bayhaqi, Abu al-Fadl, 116–117
Bedouins, 26, 30, 33, 37, 45, 46, 49, 103, 146
ben Badis, 'Abd al-Hamid, 196
bin Laden, Osama, 211
al-Biruni, 116
Bistami, Abu Yazid, 108
Black Death, 156
British colonialism, 190–191
al-Bukhari, 92

Buyids/Buwayhids, 108–110, 114, 115, 117, 121, 123, 154
Byzantines, 16, 21, 28, 32, 53–54, 58, 65, 67, 68, 69, 82, 97, 98, 100, 103, 111, 121, 122, 127, 128, 142, 159, 160

C

Cairo, 15, 100, 101, 123, 136, 139, 140, 149, 152, 154
caliphs/caliphate, 14, 29, 48, 49, 51, 61, 63, 64, 65, 67, 70, 74, 75, 76, 89, 90, 94, 95, 100, 104, 108, 109, 110, 112, 116, 117–118, 122, 160, 166, 194
Çelebi, Evliya, 163
Çelebi, Kâtip, 163
Chagatai, 136, 143, 171, 172
Christianity, 12, 14, 15, 20, 24, 25, 27, 32, 34, 38, 44, 45, 48–50, 54, 60, 66, 67, 68, 71, 73, 81, 87, 88, 96, 97, 112, 127–133, 137, 142, 149, 151, 152, 158, 159, 160, 161, 163, 168, 178, 180, 187
Christian Reconquista, 127–128, 151, 178
Companions of the Prophet, 43, 49
Constantinople/Istanbul, 16, 27, 82, 142, 159, 163
Crusaders/Crusades, 15, 68, 120, 127–133

D

dan Fodio, Usman, 190
Dara Shikoh, 174
dhimmah, 14, 44, 67, 71, 74
al-Din, Hasan, 183
Ditch, Battle of the, 44, 45

Dome of the Rock, 67, 68
Druze, 102

E

Egypt, Islam in, 89, 100–102, 128,
146, 157, 158, 160, 195,
197–198, 204, 205
Egyptian Islamic Jihad, 205
Esfahan, 169, 170
Europeans, worldwide expansion
and domination of, 156–157,
184, 185–186

F

al-Farabi, 103
al-Fasi, Muhammad 'Allal, 196
Fatah, 206
Fatimah, 59, 99, 101
Fatimids, 15, 96, 99, 100–102,
103, 108, 109, 121, 123, 128,
130, 131, 133, 146
Ferdowsi, 114
fitnahs, 61–66, 67, 73–76,
87–92
Five Pillars of Islam, 12, 68–69
Fivers, 78
Franks, 120, 127–133

G

Gandhi, Mohandas K.
(Mahatma), 174
Genghis Khan, 16, 133, 134–135,
136, 137, 144, 170
al-Ghazali, 123–126, 149
Ghazan, Mahmud, 139
Ghaznavids, 109, 114–117, 118,
121, 124, 137
Golden Horde, 136

H

Habsburgs, 161, 165, 169
Hadith, 12, 70, 85, 86, 88–89, 91,
92, 104, 105, 106, 110, 117,
150, 188, 190, 198
Hafsids, 152, 158
al-Hakim, 100–102
al-Hallaj, 104, 107–108
al-Hamadhani, 113
Hamas, 207
Hamdanids, 103, 108, 109
Hanbali, 105, 141
Harun al-Rashid, 80, 81, 82–83,
87, 124
Hezbollah, 207
Hijrah, 13, 20, 39, 56, 107
Hilalian invasion, 146
History of Prophets and Kings,
106–107
Holy League, 165
Hülegü, 136
al-Husayn, 14, 63, 167–168
Husayn I, 170

I

Ibn 'Abd Allah ibn Hasan II,
Idris, 79
Ibn al-'Arabi, 151, 153, 174, 182
Ibn al-Muqaffa', 84
Ibn al-Nafis, 140
Ibn Battutah, 153
Ibn Fadlan, 94
Ibn Hanbal, Ahmad, 88, 89,
110, 141
Ibn Hazm, 97
Ibn Hisham, 88
Ibn Ishaq, 75, 88

Ibn Khaldun, 154–155, 185
Ibn Khallikan, 140
Ibn Rushd (Averroës), 151
Ibn Saʻud, ʻAbd al-ʻAziz, 194
Ibn Saʻud, Muhammad, 189
Ibn Tashufin, Yusuf, 148–149
Ibn Taymiyyah, 140–141, 189, 190
Ibn Tufayl, 151
Ibn Tughluq, Muhammad, 139
Ibn Tumart, 149–151
Ibn Yasin, ʻAbd Allah, 148, 149, 150
Idrisids, 108, 178
Il-Khans, 136, 137
Imamis, 78, 166, 167
Imazighen, 96, 98, 133, 146–155
India, Islamic dynasties in, 115,
    116, 117, 139, 143, 146, 157,
    159, 172
Indian Ocean Islam, 158, 159,
    181–183, 190
Indo-Timurids, 157, 169, 170–178
Internet, and Islam, 208, 210
Iqbal, Sir Muhammad, 192
Iran
    Islam in, 73, 89, 113–117, 121, 143,
        157, 158–159, 166–169, 186–187,
        200–201, 202–204, 206
    as Islamic republic, 169, 170,
        203–204
Iranian Revolution, 17, 200–201,
    202–204, 206
Iraq
    cultural flowering in, 104–108
    Islamic dynasties in, 73, 80,
        89, 108–113, 121, 157,
        158–159, 162
Iraq War (2003), 211
al-ʻIsfahani, Abu ʻIsa, 65
Iskandar Muda, 181

Islam
    activism and, 55, 56, 188,
        189–190, 191
    conflicts within, 60–66, 73–79,
        80, 87–89, 93
    contributions to world
        culture, 11–12, 14–15, 81–84,
        97, 100, 103, 104–107, 114,
        116–117, 140, 141–142,
        169–170
    division of, 14, 77–79, 157
    founding/rise of, 11, 13, 36, 37,
        38–48, 49
    and globalization, 209–212
    "modern" period of, 184–213
    and a national culture,
        193–196
    and political centralization, 157
    politicizing of, 193–194, 196,
        198–199, 200–209
    precursors of, 19–28
    Renaissance of, 94
    spread of, 11, 13, 14–16, 19,
        52–54, 55–58, 60–61, 65–66,
        69–72, 90, 94–95, 152–155,
        157–159
    and structure of premodern
        society, 110–113
    and technology, 208
Islamist movements
    dimensions of revivalism,
        207–209
    mainstreaming of, 205–207
    since the 1960s, 200–205
Ismaʻil, 78, 99
Ismaʻil I, 166–167, 168
Ismaʻilis/Ismaʻiliyyah, 78, 98,
    100, 101, 102, 114, 123, 125,
    128, 133, 136, 173

J

Jacobites, 173
Ja'far al-Sadiq, 77–78
Ja'far the Barmakid, 82, 83
Jahangir, 174, 176, 177
al-Jahiz, 84, 92
Jains, 173
Jama'i-Sunnis, 77, 89, 99, 100, 107,
    109, 110, 123, 141, 149, 167
Janissaries, 143, 172, 188
Jerusalem, 15, 40, 44, 58, 67, 128,
    129, 131–132, 133, 149
Jesuits, 173
jihad, 55, 130, 148, 178, 180, 188,
    189, 190, 191–192
John (János Zápolya), 161
Judaism, 12, 14, 15, 20, 24, 27, 32,
    34, 38, 39, 44, 45, 48–50, 54,
    65, 67, 68, 71, 73, 81, 86–87,
    137, 152, 159, 173
al-Junayd, Abu al-Qasim, 108

K

Ka'bah, 30, 34, 37, 38, 47
Kamil, Mustafa, 193
Karim Khan Zand, 187
Kemal, Mustafa (Atatürk), 197
Khadijah (Muhammad's wife), 13,
    35, 36, 39
Khalid, 'Amr, 208
Kharijites, 64, 65, 73, 79, 89, 99
Khayr al-Din, 162
al-Khayzuran, 82
Khomeini, Ruhollah, 166, 201,
    202–204, 208
al-Khwarizmi, 81–83
Kishk, Sheikh, 208
Knights of St. John, 161, 162

Köprülüs, 165
Kublai Khan, 136
al-Kurani, Ibrahim, 182

L

Liu Zhi, 182

M

madrasahs (medreses), 122–125,
    163, 169
al-Maghili, 180
Maghrib, Islam in, 72, 89, 96–99,
    146, 147, 151, 152, 153, 154, 157,
    158, 160, 194–196
al-Mahdi, 82, 84, 173
Mahmud, 114–116, 117
Mahmud of Qandahar, 170
Majid, Nurcholis, 212
Majlisi, Muhammad Baqir, 170
Malik ibn Anas, 85
Malik-Shah, 122, 124–125
Mamluks, 101, 102, 133, 136, 139,
    140, 141, 143, 152, 154, 158, 160
al-Ma'mum, 83, 87–88, 89
Manmati, 176
Mansu Musa, 152, 153
Marinids, 152, 158
Marwan, 'Abd al-Malik ibn, 65,
    67–68, 69
Marwanids, 67–69, 72, 73, 74, 75,
    76, 80, 84, 95, 122
Marxism, 200, 201
Mas'ud I, 94, 117
al-Mawardi, 117–118
al-Mawdudi, Abu al-A'la, 204
Mecca, 28, 29, 36, 37, 38, 39, 42,
    43, 44, 45, 55, 63, 79, 93, 100,
    107, 174, 200

as birthplace of Muhammad, 12, 13
as centre of trade, 30, 34
and *hajj*, 30, 44, 47, 90, 99, 125, 148, 149, 153
and the Quaraysh, 30–32, 33–34, 44, 46–47, 59, 63
Medina (Yathrib), 13, 20, 28, 29, 43, 45, 47, 48, 49, 55, 58, 59, 93, 100, 125, 148
Muhammad's emigration to, 39–44, 56, 75, 107
Mehmed I, 158
Mehmed II, 159
migration, periods of, 119–120, 154–155
militancy, 199
Mir Damad, 169–170
Mirza, 'Umar Shaykh, 170
Mohammed Reza Shah Pahlavi, 202, 203
Möngke, 136
Mongols, 15, 120, 133–145, 160, 166, 171
neo-Mongols, 120, 143, 159
Mu'awiyah I, 14, 61, 63, 64–65
Mubarak, Hosni, 199, 206
Mughals (Indo-Timurids), 16, 146, 157, 169, 170–178
Muhammad, 50, 51, 53, 55, 59, 61, 63, 65, 67, 68, 70, 71, 74, 75, 77, 85, 86, 88, 89, 90, 101, 105, 106, 107, 110, 147, 150, 174, 178, 179, 190, 193, 194, 195, 212
death of, 47–48
life of, 13, 34–46
receives revelations, 11, 12, 13–14, 35–36, 37, 44, 57
and rise of Islam, 36–47, 49, 56, 59
Mullah Sadra, 169–170
Mumtaz Mahal, 176
Murad I, 142–143
Murad IV, 165
Musaylimah, 49
Muslim Brotherhood, 194, 197–199, 204, 205
Muslim Ibn al-Hajjaj, 92
Muslim World League, 200
Mustafa, 162
al-Mutanabbi, 103
al-Mu'tasim, 87, 89
al-Mutawakkil, 89
Mu'tazilah, 87–88, 89, 104–105, 109

N

Nadir Shah, 187
Naima, Mustafa, 163
Napoleon, 184, 188
al-Nasir, 133
Nasr al-Din, tales of, 177–178
Nasser, Gamal Abdel, 198, 199, 204
nationalism, and Islam, 191, 193, 196, 197–198, 206, 208
New Persian, use of, 94, 113, 114, 115, 116, 140, 158
Nile-to-Oxus region, 23–25, 53, 70, 72, 73, 154, 173
Nizam al-Mulk, 122–123, 124–125
Nizar, 123, 128, 133
al-Nuqrashi, Mahmud Fahmi, 198
Nur al-Din (Nureddin), 130–133
Nur Jahan, 176

O

Oghuz Turks, 120–121, 142
Ögödei, 135
oil production, 17, 191, 200
Osman I, 142
Ottoman language, 163
Ottomans, 16, 102, 142–143, 156,
    157, 158, 159–165, 166, 167,
    169, 170, 171, 172, 173,
    174–175, 178, 187–188, 193
    end of the empire, 194, 197
    and Westernization,
    187–188, 191

P

Pan-Islamism, 188, 192, 193
patronage, importance of in
    premodern Islamic society,
    111–112
Persian language, use of, 140, 158,
    163, 169

Q

Qadiriyah, 126
al-Qaedam 210–211
Qajars, 187, 191
al-Qalqashandi, 140
Qaramitah, 98
Qur'an, 12, 43, 49, 59, 64, 67,
    70, 71, 85, 86, 87, 88, 102,
    104, 105–106, 107, 112, 117,
    150, 151, 182, 189, 190, 198,
    201, 208
Qur'an Commentary, 106
Quaraysh tribe, 30–32, 33, 38, 39,
    40, 44, 46–47, 59, 60–61, 63
Qutb, Sayyid, 199, 204

R

Ramadan, 12, 44
Rashid al-Din, 139
Rashid Rida, Muhammad,
    193–194, 195–196
al-Razi, Abu Bakr, 114
Richard I, 132
Roman Empire, 27, 28, 53, 58, 97
Rumfa, Muhammad, 180
Rumi, Jalal al-Din, 11, 141, 174
Rum Seljuqs, 141, 142

S

el-Sadat, Anwar, 200, 205
Sa'dis, 178, 179
Safavids, 16, 157, 162, 165–170, 171,
    173, 174–175, 187
Safi al-Din, Shaykh, 165–166
Saladin, 15, 101, 129, 131–132, 133
Salafiyyah movement, 192–193
salat, 46, 57, 75
Samanids, 109, 113–114, 116
Samarkand, 144, 145, 146, 171
Sanhajah confederation, 147–148
Sasanians, 20, 21, 25, 26–27,
    53–54, 58, 67, 68, 69, 80, 106
Saudi regime, 189, 191, 197, 200,
    206–207
Sayf al-Dawlah, 103
Sebüktigin, 114
Selim (son of Süleyman), 162
Selim I (father of Süleyman), 161,
    162, 167
Selim III, 188
Seljuqs, 95, 109, 117, 118, 120–123,
    124–127, 128, 130, 136, 137,
    141, 160

September 11, 2001, terrorist attacks, 11, 210–211
Seveners, 78
al-Shafi'i, Abu 'Abd Allah, 85–86, 140
Shah Jahan, 16, 174, 176–177
Shari'ah, 85–87, 90, 107, 108, 111, 112, 126, 137, 139, 140, 141, 142, 149, 159, 160, 170, 174, 179, 180, 190, 197, 206, 207
Shari'ati, 'Ali, 201
Shi'at 'Ali, 14, 76
Shi'ites, 14, 16, 76, 77–79, 80, 85, 89, 98, 99, 100, 101, 103, 108, 109, 110, 113, 114, 115, 117, 125, 131, 137, 141, 150, 157, 165–166, 167–168, 169–170, 173, 178, 179, 187, 191, 192, 202–203
Siffin, Battle of, 63, 64–65
Sinan, 163
Sirhindi, Shaykh Ahmad, 174
Six-Day War, 200
society, structure of premodern Islamic, 110–113
sub-Saharan Africa, Islam in, 98, 152–153
Sufis, 74, 90, 92, 107–108, 121, 125, 126, 127, 139, 140, 141, 142, 165, 166, 168, 173, 174, 178, 183, 188–189, 190
Süleyman I, 160–163, 172–173
Sunnah, 36, 38, 55, 67, 70, 77, 86, 88, 89, 90–91, 105, 189, 190, 208
Sunnis, 14, 77–79, 85–86, 89, 92, 99, 100, 101, 105, 107, 113, 115, 121, 123, 125, 131, 136, 137, 141, 149, 157, 165, 167, 187, 199
al-Suyuti, 180

Syria
  Crusaders in, 128–129, 133
  Islam in, 63, 73, 103, 121, 143, 157, 158, 160, 195

T

al-Tabari, 104, 105–107
Taha Husayn, 196
Tahmasp, 168
Taj Mahal, 11, 16, 174, 176
al-Tanukhi, 113
Tanzimat, 191
tariqah fellowships, 126–127, 141, 165, 166, 173, 188, 192
Tariq ibn Ziyad, 72
terrorism, 11, 210–211
Third Worldism, 200
Thousand and One Nights, The, 11, 82, 177
Timbuktu, 152, 158, 180–181
Timur (Tamerlane), 119, 143–146, 156, 158, 159, 167, 170, 171, 172
Timurids, 157, 159, 178
Toghrïl Beg, 121
trans-Saharan Islam, 157, 178–181
Tukulor, 189
Tulip Period, 187, 188
Turks, migration/power of, 120–127, 133–143, 158–159, 171
Twelvers, 78

U

'Ubayd Allah, 99
Ulugh Beg, 145–146
'Umar I, 51, 55, 56–57, 58, 59–60, 148
'Umar II, 74

Umayyads, 15, 43, 52, 63–65, 69, 72, 73, 75, 80, 89, 95–97, 106
Usamah ibn Munqidh, 129
'Uthman ibn 'Affan, 57, 58–59, 60, 61, 63, 64

V

Vijayanagar, 159

W

Wadud, Amina, 212
al-Wahhab, Muhammad ibn 'Abd, 189
Wahhabism, 141, 189
Wali Allah, Shah, 190
al-Walid, Khalid ibn, 49, 55
waqf, 111–112
women, and Islam, 85, 102, 150, 174, 177, 202, 203, 209, 212

World Wars, 191, 193, 196, 198, 209

Y

Yahya ibn Ibrahim, 147–148
Yahya the Barmakid, 82
Yazid I, 63, 167
Young Ottomans, 191
Young Turk Revolution, 193

Z

zakat, 43, 49
Zangi, 129–130
Zápolya, János (John), 161
Zaydiyyah/Zaydis, 78, 100
Ziri, 146
Zoroastrian-Mazdeism, 25, 27, 54, 71, 80, 173
al-Zubayr, 'Abd Allah ibn, 63, 65